TOLD BY
THE PEAT FIRE

Stories by Sibylle Alexander

Merry Christmas, '02
Mom !
♡
Love, Melissa & Trevor

Hawthorn Press

Published by Hawthorn Press, Hawthorn House, 1 Lansdown Lane, Stroud, Gloucestershire, GL5 1BJ, UK
Tel: (01453) 757040 Fax: (01453) 751138

Cover Design by Patrick Roe, Southgate Solutions Ltd, Stroud, Glos.
Cover illustration by Marije Rowling
Illustrations by Gertrud Pfeiffer
Typesetting by Hawthorn Press, Stroud, Glos
Printed in the UK by Redwood Books, Trowbridge, Wiltshire

British Library Cataloguing in Publication Data applied for

ISBN 1 869 890 23X

Contents

Foreword

Ireland has been called the last remnant of paradise where no snakes can be found and where elemental beings still live in fairy hills. Their power is great, they can foresee the future and warn those among men who believe in them, like the foolish potter or Katriona in the story "Rewarded Faithfulness". They can help to build a dwelling out of love and compassion in the fairy wood, Tullynashee. The veil between the spiritual world and us becomes very thin and a child born on Midsummer Day is given the Second Sight.

Great wisdom and humour have been woven into these ancient stories of which some reach back to the Great Flood while others stem from Druidic traditions. Some were told by bards during long winter nights and they retain the power to grant wealth and happiness, obedient children and harmony in the house to the listeners.

Today's revival of the art of storytelling is a sign that people remember the rich and splendid heritage of the past and discover fresh inspiration to create new stories. My gratitude goes to Duncan Williamson and to the members of Edinburgh's Guid Crack Storytelling Club at the Netherbow and to Judy Steel from Aikwood Towers in the Borders.

Sibylle Alexander, Galashiels

Introduction

This book is dedicated to my father whose stories made the world of gnomes and fairies real to me; to Adam Bittleston who led his listeners into the realm of Celtic Christianity and interpreted the Carmina Gadelica for us, and to my five children and twelve grandchildren with their hunger for stories.

Some stories in this collection are perhaps 2000 years old, as: How Heavy is a Snowflake, which go back to the Druids; some stem from the time of early Celtic Christianity, for example The Bird's Last Supper, and The Worst of All Weathers. The much-loved Tale of the Cauldron, has come from the Scottish Highlands and I've tried to keep its archaic flavour.

Midsummers Child was first published in the Theosophical Review before 1915 and has since been retold many times before a live audience and never failed to move its hearers deeply. My gratitude goes to Michael Wood whose imagination enabled his readers to understand the dreams of a Gaelic speaking child as well as the mind of the Puritan in Belfast. May this new version help the warring parties in Northern Ireland to live in peace with each other!

From a brief notice about a midwife during the Irish famine evolved the story Rewarded Faithfulness which is highly significant for our time. The stories Nr. 6, 7, and 9, are beautiful traditional tales.

The germ for two stories, The Heather Princess, and The Foolish Potter, can be found in my very early childhood memories, yet they only began to grow when I moved to Scotland.

We live in an age of spiritual hunger and every time Duncan Williamson tells stories at the Guid Crack Storytelling Club in Edinburgh he begins by saying: "I've often gone to bed hungry but never without a story!" He was a member of the Scottish travelling people originally from Argyllshire and has saved countless oral narratives from oblivion. Now in his eighties, he gave me permission to retell The King and the Lamp, a tale every politician in our new Scottish parliament should take to heart.

Another famous story with a message is The Luckless one. A fable in in similar vein appeared even in China. It creates a lot of laughter wherever it is told and anybody trying to learn the Art of Storytelling may well begin here. Most difficult and yet rewarding to tell is the House in Tullynashee, which speaks of the limitless power possessed by The Good People, also known as the wee folk or fairies. It comes from Ireland and contains all the magic of the green island.

Return of the Brother, and The Mirror, are my own original contributions towards bridging the gap between ancient and modern consciousness, an acceptance of the ideas of reincarnation and the Second Sight in our time. The poems and prayers in this edition all stem from the Carmina Gadelica, published by Floris Books, Edinburgh.

1

1. Midsummer Child

Far away in the West of Europe, alone in a gentle bay on the white sands of Munster, stood the house of Patrick O'Hare the fisherman. It was surrounded by a garden and hedges. A goat nibbled the fresh grass, bees were searching for nectar among the heather, and wild roses blossomed in the shelter of an old apple tree.

Inside the cottage the peatfire was burning in spite of the heat, a kettle simmered and hissed. A young wife was in the last stages of labour and the midwife whispered: 'The tide is rising, it is time for your child to be born. Soon the sun will reach his highest point and Uriel reigns in the heavens'.

Patrick was holding Fiona's shoulders and he watched with awe and astonishment as the child left the womb. Its breast filled with air to send its first cry into the world and to the young mother it sounded like jubilation. 'A boy! I knew it would be a boy and we will call him John.'

Tenderly Fiona touched the head and traced the form of the tiny ears. She dipped her finger in a honeypot and let the child suck its sweetness. From the window appeared a bee as messenger from the hive and circled round the bed and the cradle to tell the queen bee an heir had been born. Patrick measured the length of the shadows on the floorboards, then walked into the garden to mark the highest hill, where the line between light and darkness showed the time of day. He nodded: yes indeed, it was the hour of Uriel, the guardian of truth, who brings the second sight as a blessing to those born in midsummer.

All the tension of the long hours of waiting slipped away and he shouted to the old she-goat: 'Listen Nanny Goat!

We have got a son, our dream has come true.' Three times the Irishman circled the house murmuring old Gaelic runes, drawing down blessings on mother and child. Then he hastened down to the beach where his friend Angus had been waiting to hear the news. 'Our Johnny has been born and he is as fair and frail as Fiona. Will you be his godfather? We will take him to church when he is strong enough for the voyage.' 'That I will gladly do for you, but before I speak to the priest let us give the child the old blessing here and now.'

They found Fiona asleep with her child in her arms. The midwife joined the two men when they spoke the ancient rune of baptism:

> The little drop of the Father on thy little forehead, beloved one.
> The little drop of the Son on thy little forehead, beloved one.
> The little drop of the Spirit on thy little forehead, beloved one.
> A wavelet for thy form, a wavelet for thy voice, a wavelet for thy sweet speech.
> A wavelet for thy luck, a wavelet for thy good, a wavelet for thy health.
> A wavelet for thy throat, a wavelet for thy pluck, a wavelet for thy graciousness,
> Nine wavelets for thy graciousness.

The sign of the cross sealed the blessing; Angus returned to his boat and soon disappeared behind the cliffs.

John grew up into a slender, fair-haired boy with large grey eyes and though he remained an only child he felt no loneliness, even when Patrick was away on the sea. He had friends among the seals and dolphins, the heath was populated with the Little People, elves and fairies, a wee brownie lived in the bothy and received his share of milk at night. As long as he was there no sickness could touch men or beasts. Johnny loved to tease the sullen leprechaun and tried in vain to snatch his red cap, for every child knows he has to lead you to the crock of gold, buried at the foot of the rainbow, if you possess his cap. Then his father would never need to sail away...

Fiona could not see the Little People but she trusted her son's vision to be true and loved to hear his accounts of their activities. Few other people ever came to the lonely shore. Neither priest nor school teacher fathomed what the grey eyes of this child perceived when on rare feast days the family sat at church. Johnny was taught by his mother both in Gaelic and English but all his dreams were in the old tongue and he learnt many stories and legends from her as well as hundreds of songs and poems. But terrifying images came sometimes with the gift of the second sight, images that haunted him whenever a ship had been dashed to pieces on the cliffs. With his inner eyes he saw the drowning men and he could not cope with it till the old midwife came and comforted him. 'Dead are these sailors, dead and without a grave, and they come to you and implore you to fold your hands and speak to God as there is nobody else who could pray for them. No priest has blessed them, no candles have been lit and they need your mediation. Speak the old runes for their souls and when you come to the end of your own long life you will find many friends in the Land of Truth waiting for you.'

After a terrible storm which caused havoc she gave him a small cross carved from the wood of a rowan tree and taught him a prayer to Saint Michael the Archangel, and the song of Brendan, the sea-loving saint. 'Oh Johnny, Death is a merciful Lord, tenderly he rocks these who drown at sea. Praying is a holy office: Christ carries the prayers to God on High and to the Choirs of Angels. Among all tongues Gaelic is most

5

precious and sounds sweetest in the ears of Jesus because Brigit sang her songs during his first night here on earth.

O God of the Elements, O God of the mysteries, O God of the fountains, Oh King of Kings, O King of kings!

Thy joy the joy, thy light the light, thy war the war, thy peace the peace, thy peace the peace.

Thy pain the pain, thy love the love, that lasts for aye, to the end of ends, to the end of ends.

Thou pourest Thy grace on those in distress, on those in straits, without stop or stint, without stop or stint.

Thou Son of Mary, thou Son of Grace, who wast and shalt be, with the ebb, with the flow, with the ebb and flow.

When John turned nine he was a bright and alert child, yet full of dreams; interested in everything around him and yet happiest at night when he sat at the peatfire and his mother told him stories from Ireland while turning her spinning wheel. Whenever Patrick came home there was a fine celebration with song and laughter. Fresh fried fish and bannocks, elderberry wine and honey cakes while Patrick told of his adventures. He always brought presents in his pockets, a piece of silk or a comb for Fiona, toys or books to read. Love lived among them but their happiness was to end abruptly.

The worst gale in living memory blew up over the Atlantic ocean in late September, and Patrick was out in his boat. Fiona climbed the hill behind the house with John following behind. They strained their eyes to catch a glimpse of him but all they saw were miles of roaring waves. Then the clouds ripped apart and against a slate

grey backdrop John saw the gigantic wings of St. Michael
who held a light in his hands, the sign of death. 'Oh Holy
Michael, protect my father!' he shouted into the wind
before a violent gust threw him down. He gasped for
breath and when he looked westwards the vision faded.
The hurricane pressed Fiona hard against the rock and
she struggled to reach her child. The descent was
difficult, heavy rain soaked them to the skin and the fire
was out when finally they reached home. The wind
howled in the chimney and in vain did they try to kindle
a flame. They crept into bed without supper, comforting
each other. In a dream John saw his father and heard his
voice: 'Farewell my son, forgive me that I call your
mother. We need each other in death. Farewell.'

The storm lasted for three days. Fiona stayed in bed with a
high temperature and if the wee Brownie had not lent a hand
the fire would never have been lit. John milked the goat but
apart from that there was little food. He did not dare to give
the message from his father but in her delirium she seemed
to speak with him. When at last the wind died down her soul
flew into the Land of Truth and John was left alone.

Angus found the child next to his dead mother, completely
stunned with grief. His godfather coaxed him to take a meal
and tell what had happened. Among the papers he found an
address of Fiona's brother in Belfast, the only relative.
Before Johnny had packed his belongings the old midwife
came, guardian of his childhood, and she spoke the ancient
verses which every mother would give her child on the first
journey away from home:

> Dark is yonder town, Dark are those therein
> Thou art the brown swan, Going in among them
> Their hearts are under thy control, Their tongues are
> beneath thy soul
> Nor will they ever utter a word to give thee offence

But John did not understand. He understood nothing anymore, his world had collapsed. The wise woman pushed the verse into his pocket and gave him her blessing.

Shy and vulnerable and as a stranger the child entered the family of James Mackai, a puritan. He had four children, Collin was sixteen and the apple of his father's eye. Three sisters, all younger than John, were valued little and all of them were brought up in strict fashion. The mother was a silent woman who never sang or laughed; she undertook the care of this nephew as a duty and without love or affection. James Mackai held an important office in the city and was deemed an honest man, but he had few friends.

John had to attend the Protestant school. Here he sat silently between the other boys who mocked him for his quaint dialect and did not hesitate to express their contempt for Catholics. Only at night did John find peace; in his dreams he saw his parents and the cottage with its goat and bees.

In the summer the family went on holiday to the seaside and there Johnny revived. He played with the little girls, he collected shells and built sandcastles for them. He loved the wide open sky and the high dunes. A friendship developed with Collin who enjoyed conversations with his strange cousin who held such different opinions about almost everything and had such a gentle nature. Mrs Mackai also began to appreciate the foster-son because he entertained her daughters and that gave her rare moments of peace. Only James Mackai remained sternly aloof; he had never forgiven his sister for her marriage to a papist.

On a brilliantly hot and sunny day Johnny romped with the girls in the bay and perhaps for the first time he felt completely happy and relaxed. When they felt tired he promised to tell a story and pictures rose in his soul, images of the little people, the Brownie and the

Leprechaun. The girls were hanging on his every word and at supper they talked about nothing else. 'What a nice story you invented,' the mother said and John answered innocently that he didn't invent it, it was true. 'Guard your tongue!' his uncle growled. 'In my house no lies are told and if you don't revoke what you just said I will beat you.' Terrified John looked at him; he had never been beaten in his life. The girls pleaded in vain, even their mother intervened when she saw the expression in John's wide open eyes. This incensed the man as he felt his authority was being undermined. 'Recant or else!' he shouted and fetched his stick when no answer came. He put the boy over a chair and thrashed him. Collin sprang to his defence: 'Beat me, father, but not this child who does not know what a lie is.' 'Then it is time the papist learns his lesson. I will beat him every night unless he takes his words back.'

The girls wept hysterically, John was as white as a sheet. 'The beings of which you speak do not exist or they would be mentioned in the Bible. I will not tolerate that you corrupt my children in their innocence with lies. I expect you to come to my room and apologise.'

Deeply disturbed and confused John remained silent and he was beaten every day at sunset. He hardly ate anything, Collin could not bear to see him suffer and took him aside. 'You must give in, Johnny, you simply cannot go on living like this. I know my father! You have no idea of his suffering and how it's hurting him. He regards it as his duty to break your obstinacy so that you won't go to hell. Better a beating on earth than eternal pain, says Calvin. I beg you to help him.'

The boy stared at him. What he had just heard seemed unfathomable and incomprehensible. So far he had never cried at the time of beating but now he sobbed as if his heart would break; his whole body was convulsed and it took Collin a long time to comfort him. He wiped away all traces of tears, took the child firmly into his arms and waited until John could speak again. 'You are right, I have to recant... but do you know what it means?' said John. Collin took him to the door of James Mackai's room where the man sat brooding before the Bible. Only two words were needed but nobody understood what the first conscious lie meant to this child of Uriel.

The holidays resumed their calm course till two events shook the peace of the family. Not far from their favourite beach were some high dunes and whenever John wanted to be alone he would climb up and look out over the sea. A short but violent storm had brought rain but now the sun was shining and the water was calm. John was watching the rhythm of the seaweeds when he suddenly saw a sailor with red hair and empty, staring eyes floating like a piece of driftwood. John jumped up and ran down to Collin who was fishing and told him what he had seen. Instantly Collin returned uphill and out of curiosity the three girls followed. Panting heavily they all arrived at the top of the dunes and John gave a detailed description of what he saw. 'Are you joking? There is nothing at all!' said Collin. He looked critically at his cousin and when he saw his expression he realised that John was serious. 'It seems to me that you perceive things which are not there for us. Believe me, even if you think that what you see is true the reality is different. Keep quiet if you value your life.'

Impatiently the sisters looked for the promised sensation. 'It is only a bit of seaweed, be careful of the steep shore. And promise not to breathe a word about this to anyone.' Hardly had Collin spoken when they heard the tap, tap of their father's walking-stick. John flinched and Collin put a protective arm round his shoulders and called out: 'The sailor has disappeared. Let's run a race to mother's deckchair; the first there wins.'

James Mackai looked puzzled. His nephew remained a riddle to him. But the evening paper reported on the death by drowning of a sailor called Red Freddie who had been washed overboard in the recent storm. The body had not been recovered. Collin nodded meaningfully, the parents were silent. From that day a closer bond between the two boys brought happiness to John who felt that at least one person believed in him.

The second event was far more dramatic. Collin received an invitation from a friend to attend a sporting gala in the next town, about two hours' walk away. He would stay overnight with Malcolm and return two days later. Collin packed his rucksack and departed early in the morning to strike north. The following night John dreamt of a strange tree growing at the edge of the sea, one strong branch stretching out horizontally over the water. Below the steep shore was a narrow ledge where he seemed to discern Collin writhing with pain. Abruptly John woke up and in spite of the late hour he crept to the study where a light was still burning. He knocked hesitantly and James opened the door, clearly irritated by the late visitor. When he saw the pallor in John's face he tried to cheer him up with a joke. 'Hello little man, did you see any ghosts or perhaps a leprechaun?' John saw the stick in the corner and his heart missed a beat. 'I came to ask if there is any news from Collin?' 'What do you think? He only left this morning. We expect him back tomorrow night. You should be asleep, good night.' The boy felt wretched when he climbed back to bed and hardly dared to close his eyes as the picture of tree and cliff and the lifeless form of his friend tormented him all night.

He dared not speak again till evening came and he was able to leave the family and run along the coastal path. There he met Malcolm who called out: 'Where has Collin been? We lost our game without him. Didn't he get my invitation?' He noticed the agitation in John's voice when he answered: 'Yes he did and he left early yesterday, but I was worried and wanted to search for him.' 'This is a matter for the police! You run home and raise the alarm. We must find him quickly.'

Malcolm was impatient to start the search and sent Johnny flying home. There pandemonium broke out when he mentioned Malcolm's request. In vain he begged to be allowed to join the search party; Mrs Mackai fainted and he was ordered to give the girls their supper and put them to bed. Police and neighbours fanned out to explore the wood and the coastline, darkness was falling and for John another torturous night began, when he saw his friend's suffering in ever more vivid images within his mind.

Towards morning the troop returned exhausted after a fruitless search and James Mackai locked himself into his room, refusing to eat or drink. A life without Collin, his son and heir, was devoid of any meaning for the puritan; the girls counted for next to nothing in his eyes. But John felt imprisoned by his visions; and when he also suddenly heard the voice of his friend calling for help he decided to take the matter into his own hands. Quietly he pulled on an old jacket but when his hand strayed into the pocket he found the piece of paper on which his childhood guardian had written the words: 'Dark is yonder town, dark are those therein', it suddenly made sense, particularly when he came to the line: 'Nor will they ever utter a word - to give you offence.' Courage was flooding through him and he knocked boldly at his uncle's door and faced the irate man squarely. 'Is there a tree on the way north which stretches out a long, horizontal branch out over the sea?' 'Why do you ask? Yes indeed the tree is well known as The Gallows because pirates used to be hanged there, but you have never been there.' 'I saw the tree in my dream and just below it on a narrow ledge I saw Collin and he seems to be in great pain.' The heavy man turned abruptly away and paced up and down the room, his mind in turmoil. Could it be that the strange eyes of this child saw more than others? Then he took a decision. He fetched blankets, a strong rope and a potion, sent a message to the police and set off with Johnny at a fast pace.

It was dark among the trees, only starlight reflected from the sea, and it took them almost an hour before they reached the spot where an ancient oak tree stretched its branch across the water. The moment John saw it he felt absolutely certain and hope to save his friend quickened. He threw himself onto his knees and bent to look over the sheer cliff. Indeed there was a ledge jutting out and on it lay the motionless figure of Collin. James called to his son, a moan was the answer. The boy was still alive but he was very weak and his leg was broken. Lowering the rope they both tried to tie it round Collin's waist and by the time they succeeded the police had arrived with more ropes and a stretcher. Together they pulled up Collin who had suffered terrible pain, but worse than the broken leg had been his thirst. Surrounded by water he would have perished if another night had passed without help. After a long drink he found his voice: 'How did you find me? Twice people walked past and I shouted till I was hoarse but the noise of the sea drowned any sound. I had reached the point that I wanted to roll into the sea rather than spend another night thirsting.' James took him into his arms and said: 'It was Johnny who told us where you were. He led us to The Gallow tree but how on earth he knew about it is a mystery to me.' Then Collin's face lit up: 'I called him! Over and over again I called for Johnny.'

When they returned home Mrs Mackai had hot soup ready and everybody was invited, Malcolm and all the weary searchers celebrated Collin's rescue and praised Johnny. The boy looked around the table, saw the girls in their night-dresses, his uncle beaming at Collin who had recovered sufficiently to enjoy the meal, a tender look from his aunt, and suddenly he knew: this was now his family, he belonged.

He slept deeply and without any dreams; the breakfast table was decorated with wild flowers which the girls had picked for him and the mother said kindly: 'When you have eaten, Johnny, go to Uncle James, he has a surprise for you.' Never before had he seen such warm love in her eyes. Without fear he knocked at the door. James gave him a signet ring: 'This is a token of our gratitude, Collin would not have survived much longer and we owe you his rescue. But tell me, why did you come to my room the first night after Collin left?' John hung his head and confessed reluctantly that he had seen the Gallow tree and the cliffs with a figure below even then. 'And you were too afraid of me to talk about it?' Deeply agitated, James Mackai walked up and down the room till he suddenly came to stand in front of the walking stick, took it and broke it in two. 'Never again shall you be afraid in my house. Oh, how much pain and anguish I could have prevented if I had trusted you. But tell me, is there any wish you have? I will gladly fulfil it if I can.' 'No, nothing really, I've got all I need except perhaps would you allow me to tell the girls that I did not lie to them?' Very quietly and yet with great emphasis the puritan said: 'Yes Johnny, that you may and I myself will be with you. Come, we'll go together.'

2. Return of the Brother

Not far from the Boyne near the old monastery of Clonard lived a boy with the name of Peter who could not walk. His mother thought he had been born too early, before he had been complete, and the boy thought that the angels didn't have time to stitch up his back properly and that's why there was a hole.

Peter was a bright and intelligent child who brought great joy to his parents. Strange and indeed unforgettable were his shining large grey-blue eyes with a dark ring round the iris; nobody had ever seen such brilliant eyes. His home was a rambling old house, its garden was a bird paradise and it stretched down to the river. The large hall was often used for concerts, as both parents were musicians and their many friends loved to play for a child so keen on listening and with such love for the music of old masters. Only the song of birds competed with their friends' music-making, as the windows stood wide open whenever possible.

When wee Sebastian was born the joy of Peter knew no bounds, and he rejoiced that his brother was whole and well. But it took time until the baby grew into a boy with whom he could play and throughout those early years the cradle and later a cot stood next to Peter's bed or in a pram close to his wheelchair. Sebastian's first memory was that of two bright eyes gazing down at him.

After six years there came a long hot summer Sebastian would remember throughout his life as a time of great happiness. A special deckchair had been built for Peter which had four wheels, enabling the boy to lie low near the ground and move around in the garden. The brothers built small houses with bark and covered the roofs with moss, laid paths paved with gravel, dug mini-flowerbeds, made fields of green cress and planted wild strawberries. Sebastian enjoyed running to fetch whatever Peter suggested and their games filled many hours. At night Peter would invent stories about the Little People who lived in the miniature village.

Then Peter had to go into hospital in Dublin and he grew despondent. A shadow lay over his face when his father visited him and when asked what was wrong he shook his head: 'It's no use telling you, nobody can make my wish come true.' Finally he confessed how he longed to hear birdsong and the rushing of the river and the wind in the treetops, all the sounds of home. 'If you could play such music to me I could imagine I was playing our favourite game in the garden.'

From then on his father never went anywhere without a notebook in his pocket and he would stop and listen to various bird calls and write down the music. At his next visit Peter had to guess to which bird the tunes belonged. Though they had great fun together something was still missing and tentatively Peter asked whether all the melodies could be woven together as in nature where everything formed one harmony. Thoughtfully the father walked home along the river busily composing a concert.

Peter's homecoming was like a festival: neighbours and friends had been invited with their instruments to play The Symphony of Nature for him. Violins sang their summer song, silver flutes gave voice to different birds, a viola hummed like a swarm of bees and the cello provided a never-ceasing rush of water while a glockenspiel chimed its tinkling joy. Each instrument was given a solo, the piano wove all the tunes together in a wonderful harmony. The boys clapped and demanded an encore; the friends were well rewarded by their shining faces.

It seemed as if Peter lived with a heightened awareness of everything around him. He watched the clouds shaping and reshaping. His frail body recorded each change in the weather as if it was an instrument tuned too finely. The hot summer was followed by a great and splendid autumn with wide, clear skies. Sudden storms broke out and Peter had to remain indoors but when he heard the hard cry of wild geese his father had to carry him out into the fields where he watched their flight southward. In winter the boys spent many hours painting together, Peter with delicate pastel colours, Sebastian using strong, bright paints. His brother watched the effort and remarked: 'You can't make a picture only with bright colours, everything has a shadow you know. It is just the same as in music; it would be boring to play only in a major key. Joys and sorrows belong together.' But Sebastian did not understand him yet.

During Lent Peter's strength seemed to slip away; he would lie quietly against his pillow while Sebastian tried hard to cheer him up with the first spring flowers: celandine and snowdrops, cuckoo flower, cowslip and periwinkle. Easter came with glorious warm sunshine and butterflies danced in the soft breeze but still the boy was too weak for the traditional egg hunt in the garden. And so the coloured eggs were hidden in the hall and Peter was given a long goose feather to point to places where he guessed the eggs were hidden. Sebastian collected them in a basket to be shared out during the festive Easter breakfast.

'May I hear the Symphony of Nature once more?' Peter asked, and with great effort the musicians were brought together on the same evening. It was as if summer had come when the house was filled with birdsong and the humming of bees, yet the players had tears in their eyes when they looked at the boy with his pale face and a far-away expression in his large eyes. A restless night followed, the doctor was called and when he left at dawn Sebastian crept into the sickroom.

'Peter', he began fearfully, 'why does mummy cry in the kitchen?' 'I will tell you if you promise not to cry yourself!' Fervently the child promised and crossed his heart. 'You know that when your next birthday comes along you will be eight and then nine and then ten, but I will never ever be more than twelve.' Sebastian looked mystified: 'What do you mean? No more birthdays for you?' Peter searched for an explanation then his face lit up. 'Let me draw a picture for you and then you will know exactly what I mean.'

Sebastian ran to fetch paper and crayons, then looking for a firm support he placed the picture book 'Nils Holgerson's Wonderful Journey' on the blanket and settled himself close to the bedside to watch every line and stroke. 'Here is our house with the high roof and next to it the trees...behind the Boyne...above some clouds...but look here is a hole, between the clouds, all blue. It really is an open door but grown-ups don't understand that. I tell you for sure that I am going to fly through that door into Heaven, perhaps quite soon. I had a glimpse and I'm really looking forward to going there, so it's stupid to cry.' Lowering his voice he whispered conspiratorially: 'Sebastian, I have an even bigger secret and you are the only one I trust to keep it. Look at the top left hand corner of the picture. First I'll draw a tiny wild goose, far away, then bigger and bigger ones and see how the last and biggest one is landing on the roof? That is how I will return. Just remember the wild geese.'

Utterly exhausted by the effort Peter sank back into the pillows while Sebastian carried the precious picture into his own room to hide it with care, still puzzled but feeling very proud about his brother's confidence in him.

When the light coffin was slowly carried to the cemetery Sebastian ran ahead to pick fistfuls of the last yellow primroses and he arrived just in time to throw them down to Peter into the grave, keeping the tears back as he had promised. He searched the sky for wild geese but none were to be seen. It was not yet the right time....

Many years later, long after he had left home and had found a young wife in a northern country, Sebastian was looking through some old papers when he discovered Peter's last picture, the carefully hidden secret. For a long while he mused while the dear face of his brother rose before his inner eyes and suddenly he seemed to hear his voice again saying softly: 'That is how I will return. Remember the wild geese.' Perplexed he placed the picture back into its hiding-place.

The arctic summer with its long white nights had come to an end, to be replaced by a stormy autumn. The young woman expected her first child and a cradle stood waiting in the warm, comfortable home. Sebastian was woken at midnight by the groans from his wife and then she pleaded: 'It is time for the doctor, he has a long way to walk!' Step by step Sebastian had to fight his way against a gale which blew into his face. Gradually a pale dawn appeared in the sky and he stopped to catch his breath. Suddenly he heard a strange sound getting louder and louder till he recognised the cry of wild geese and the beating of their wings. Flying in strict formation the flock headed towards his own house and further south to warmer countries. Then he remembered the Symphony of Nature and resuming his walk he sang its tunes into the wind.

It was a long struggle till the young mother gave birth and the cry of the firstborn filled the house. When the doctor placed the warm little bundle into the arms of the father he was overwhelmed by the sight and feel and touch of the tiny creature. Sebastian searched for some family features but could find nothing to remind him of anybody. With a soft crooning voice he sang the melody of birdsong, bees and river and the child stopped crying as if it was listening intently. Inhaling deeply it slowly opened its tightly screwed eyelids: two radiant, grey-blue eyes gazed up at Sebastian, the eyes of his lost brother. A wave of warmest happiness engulfed him and with tears streaming down his face he bent down to his beloved wife to share the secret of his joy.

3. Rewarded Faithfulness

Katriona was as bonny as any Irish lass could be, with auburn hair and the clearest skin the soft rains can bestow. Many of the young men in the village looked with longing at her slim figure and she never lacked dancing partners at the fair; but as she had no dowry there could be no wedding. No farmer gave his son to a penniless girl and Katriona was the youngest in her family. Not a penny for her! She trained as a midwife and moved away over the ridge of hills into a valley where she was soon indispensable. Whether she was called to a humble cottage or to a rich farmer she did her best and her strong hands could be gentle when needed. She knew how apple cider vinegar helped during pregnancy, rosemary oil massaged on the back relieved pain, and comfrey gave strength. The great joy was the moment when a new-born babe was in her arms and she would croon old Gaelic songs, looking at the child without envy. If she walked through the village the children always followed her about trying to catch her by the skirt. She would call each one by name, tenderly stroking their hair, and if she had time tell them stories.

On other days she would witness an early death of a young mother, see the despair of a father. Sometimes she was called to perform an emergency baptism and then follow a small coffin to the cemetery. It was a place she visited often, bringing flowers for the little ones that had slipped away too soon. She knew about the help elemental beings could give and in every house she made sure the brownie had its porridge at night with cream or fresh milk. Many a night when she was battling for a fragile life she called on the elves to assist her, and some of her stories were not only told for children but for the invisible creatures as well. She had an inkling that the Little People longed to hear something about small infants. She knew that elementals cannot see or perceive children before they reach the age of seven: till then they remain invisible to them. Katriona had a rich store of such tales and she shared them generously.

It was during the early autumn when the midwife sat in a large kitchen, waiting to be called upstairs. A kettle hissed, the cat was locked out in order to give the hobgoblin peace to drink his milk, when suddenly a low voice whispered into her ear: 'Katriona, in two days Clare is expecting her first child. She is hiding in the bothy behind the hedge where rosehips and sloes are ripening. Clare trusted the wicked sailor who promised to marry her but he sailed away and she is without help or hope, only you can save her.'

There was hardly time to digest the message when a call demanded immediate assistance to the plump wife who laboured long and fitfully till at last the child emerged, looking blue and lifeless; no cry lifted the small breast. Quickly Katriona filled two basins with water, one warm, one cold and dipped the boy into contrasting temperatures. Finally the lips parted, a whimper could be heard and a gentle clap brought the first cry, followed by deep gulps of air being sucked in. Anxiety and fear were replaced by joy and hope.

The rich farmer was moved to tears when he held his heir. 'No doctor could have done better than you, wish for whatever you want, Katriona,' and he pressed some coins into her hand. 'Yes I do have a wish and it can easily be fulfilled. There is another child waiting to be born and its mother lacks everything. Your wife has enough clothes for triplets, please allow me to make up a bundle of what is needed.' Her wish was granted generously, and so it came about that the midwife carried vests, jackets and nappies in one hand and a big bundle with bread, milk, butter and oats in the other. She found the path to the old bothy where red rosehips and dusty blue sloes ripened. It was as if her feet were guided by the invisible beings who had given the message.

She found a young girl huddled in a dark corner: no fire in the grate, not a scrap of food, only a jug with water for the mother-to-be. Plenty of dry wood lay outside to kindle flames in the hearth and warm some milk for Clare, who ate ravenously and thanked Katriona as if she had been an angel of mercy. Then she told her story about her sheltered childhood, her well-to-do parents and the charm of Gerry with his red-golden hair and vast promises, her complete ignorance of life and poverty, her escape into the unknown and her utter despair. Soon the cobwebs were cleared from the bothy, fresh bracken for the bed cut along the hedgerow and clean linen spread out. The birth was swift and a frail little girl with red-golden down filled the hut with what seemed unearthly light.

'Her name shall be Naomi,' said Clare, 'she has to find a home with strangers; I cannot keep her however much I long to, for she would starve to death.' As long as the provisions lasted the two women shared the bothy and picked berries in the mild sunshine. 'I know of a rich farmer in my own village back home who has a kind and generous heart. There Naomi will grow up well cared for and loved. You can return to your parents and begin a new life. The secret of Naomi will be preserved and no questions asked. Let us go there together,' said Katriona.

On the way they were given hospitality: they had buttermilk to drink, scones to eat and Naomi was thriving. The rich farmer took the child without hesitation and thanked Katriona profusely. Clare had parted from her baby and walked on before they reached the farm. Katriona went to visit her own home where only the eldest brother still lived. He urged her to move back whenever she was free to do so and she promised that she would. Meanwhile she had much work waiting for her, as Ireland's cradles are never empty for long.

Years passed and life became difficult, there was more sickness and more discontent, old traditions died and Katriona suffered greatly, unable to understand the root of the trouble. No longer did she receive the same help from the elementals - it was as if they too suffered. Neither fairies nor hobgoblins visited the village and when after a long struggle little Teresa died, Katriona walked towards the fairy knoll and sat down utterly exhausted and dispirited. Perhaps she would gain strength there or even get an answer to why God should take a life that had hardly began.

It was very quiet, no cry of birds, no humming of bees amongst the dying heather. Obeying old customs she placed pieces of cake from the funeral on the hill and closed her eyes. Remaining motionless, a faint sound reached her ear. 'Wake up, you have to listen to us.' Nobody was to be seen, an empty heath, a silent world around her. It seemed as if the fairy hill beckoned her, she moved some ivy swaying gently and found a door behind it which led into the hill. Following a downward path she saw a dim light far away, her feet found the right direction and soon she heard some flute playing. Turning the last corner she emerged into a wide hall filled with innumerable gnomes; on a throne sat their king who had a grave expression on his face. She bowed to greet him and was given a seat before him.
'Thank you for coming to us. We summoned you because you are the only one prepared to listen.'

Katriona looked around the circle of serious-faces and waited. The king continued: 'You grieved for Teresa, but soon the children of Ireland will die by their thousands.'

With her hands pressed to her heart she wailed: 'But why, what have we done?' 'You planted poison into our good soil, deadly nightshades instead of corn, potatoes and tomatoes, even tobacco plants to ruin us and yourselves. The nicotine is making men deaf and dumb to the spiritual world and blind towards us. From all over Europe processions of Little People came to find refuge on our sacred green island but now the poisons are all around us. A most devastating potato pest will wipe out the next harvest and folk will starve to death, the children first, then the old men and finally the women.

You are the only one who still remembers that we need tokens of love, food freely given and prayers spoken, and that is the reason we have called you here to utter a warning.' 'But what can I do? Being without land I can't plant anything and the farmers won't listen to a woman.' She did not doubt for a moment that the gnomes spoke the truth, yet faced with a famine she felt helpless. 'Tell all those who will listen to return to the old, safe crops of rye, barley, oats and wheat and encourage the young men to flee across the sea and start a new life.' A flute began its tune and the audience was over. Stupefied, Katriona stumbled through the long passage out into the pale sunshine and with a heavy heart she walked into the village.

At home a letter waited for her. It came from her brother who again invited her to come and live with him as his wife had died. In her answer she explained how her work demanded that she would stay a little longer but she begged him to plant only cereals, turnips and vegetables, and none of the new-fangled potatoes, and to warn his neighbours; the reason she could not explain. When she posted the letter she felt her courage return and from then on she taught mothers to use traditional food for the children and even spoke to the rich farmers. They laughed and told her to stick to her job with wives and babies, they knew best. Only the schoolmaster listened gravely as an English newspaper had mentioned the threat of the potato pest and he alerted the shopkeeper to lay in extra reserves for the winter. He also encouraged a few families to emigrate but otherwise not much did change in the valley.

Katriona observed carefully what the effects of nightshades were on humans and she noted how reverence for old people disappeared and knowledge of elementals vanished; instead of feeling respect for old traditions men were proud of new technology and English began to be spoken more and more instead of Gaelic. She was getting older, but she received none of the respect every child used to show the 'bodach', the old man or woman. No longer did the day begin and end with prayers, work was done with haste and the runes spoken before sowing the seed or harvesting the corn were forgotten. Yet what she missed most was the sheer joy and kindness among and between neighbours, the bards no longer gathered listeners around the peatfire and each person tended to think only of himself. The lilt of laughter died.

Spring came late the following year, the weather stayed wet and cold, seed potatoes were mouldy and some farmers remembered the warnings. When at last apple trees opened their blossom, ice-cold showers killed any chances for pollination and bees starved. Every potato field was blighted, starvation followed swiftly.

Much has been written about the Irish famine; over a million people lost their lives and those who survived lived on nettles, seaweeds and acorns. Cattle died and the pigs were too thin to provide much food. Those who had friends in America sailed west, leaving the old people to fend for themselves. Katriona helped as much as it was within her means and so she left it too late for her return to the valley of her childhood; winter had set in with cruel frost and biting winds. She stood with a bundle on her back facing the climb over the ridge of hills but the path was covered in thick snow. Her strength had gone and every step was an effort, the wet skirt clung to her frozen limbs and only her hope of reaching the house of the O'Briens kept her going; they lived more than halfway towards her village. Finally she collapsed in the snow and closed her eyes. And there she would have died had not the smell of peatfire reached her, conjuring up the vision of friends, food and warmth. She strained her eyes and indeed there was a faint glow of light, an open door towards which she struggled with new hope, almost falling into outstretched hands who helped her over the threshold into the warm, firelit room. Her cold hands fused around a hot cup of tea, freshly baked oatcakes appeared on the table, brown rolls with butter next to a bowl of soup. She was allowed to eat and eat undisturbed till she walked over to the boxbed and slept between clean sheets while unseen helpers dried her wet clothes and shoes.

The house was empty when Katriona awoke, refreshed from her deep sleep, and the sun shone in through the window. A glittering blanket of snow covered the familiar landscape and the wind had calmed down. A bright fire burnt in the hearth, creamy porridge bubbled in a skillet and the kettle sang its tune. A jug with rich milk stood next to her plate and Katriona thought she had never tasted a more delicious breakfast in her life. A knotted bundle with honey cakes stood ready to take with her on the journey. She saw no member of the O'Brien family but she would thank them another day now that she would live closer; perhaps they were at work in the forest, but she could behold no footsteps in the snow: they must have left very early.

With fresh energy Katriona set off, turning once more to wave back to the house...but no smoke curled against the sky. Before her the valley of her childhood opened up and she hastened her step. Her brother hardly recognised her under the heavy shawl, an old woman with sunken cheeks; only her eyes had kept the clear and direct gaze.

The village had survived the famine better thanks to Katriona's warning, though some of the older people had died and only a few children were running around. A nun had taken most of the pupils to a monastery in England, some young mothers had followed, the men had emigrated. In describing the terrible ordeal of the last few months Katriona relived the nightmare of starvation and finally came to the story of her own delivery from death in the snow. Vividly she painted a picture of the O'Briens' hospitality, the food and warmth, the snug boxbed, the rich breakfast. Her brother sat up: 'But how could that be? The house has been empty for years and the family sailed to the New World long ago!' Then he heard his sister's bright laugh as she listened to the absurd notion of having dreamt the rescue and triumphantly she waved the white cloth in which the sweet honey cakes had been. 'Here is my proof!' she laughed and her brother took the handkerchief into his rough hands. His face grew solemn as he examined the seams, pointing to the fine stitches. 'Only fairy folk can do such work; no humans gave you shelter, the Good People themselves saved your life.' Silently Katriona gazed at the embroidery and nodded. Full of awe and wonder her brother looked at her and asked seriously: 'Tell me, sister, did you get the warning of the famine from the wee folk? I was wondering, you always seemed to see and hear more than others.' She nodded but implored him to keep quiet about it, and he promised.

The weather stayed calm, and after Katriona had rested she begged her brother to visit the place of hospitality which had left an indelible image in her mind. It was not far and soon they came to the corner where the road turned downwards. Behind the trees there were just blackened ruins without door or windows, the inside yawned empty to the sky, a few burnt sticks in the cold hearth, a bundle of withered ferns in the corner where she had slept. Had it been mere deception or illusion? 'With a thousand stitches the elementals attach the visible world to the invisible heaven', said her brother, 'you have been blessed'.

Whenever any children came to her house Katriona would tell them stories and her last words always held a warning. 'Remember the brownies and hobgoblins, feed them at night with porridge and cream, but shut out the cat. Show reverence to the invisible world and never destroy a fairy hill. Be grateful to the Little People.'

Much misery followed in the wake of the potato famine; over a million lives were lost and whole villages were deserted. A few old survivors remembered the sacred sites, though, and prevented railways from being built above a fairy knoll, or telephone wires trespassing on the dwelling places of gnomes.

4. The House in Tullynashee

Among all the thousands of stories told in Ireland this one, 'The House in Tullynashee', must be one of the strangest, and it never loses its magic in the telling. My thanks go to Ruth Duffin who told it last and, if any of you are shaking your head in disbelief, she is my witness that I have followed her version as faithfully as I could. The events really happened, I am told, and they bear witness to the unlimited powers of the invisible host of elemental beings who made their home in Ireland after fleeing from the continent. The creative powers of paradise live in the remote corners of the green islands and are at work even today.

In the wee village of Kilcormac there lived three children: Patrick with his sister Eileen and their best friend Jimmy who lived next door behind a hedge. The gardens stretched out north of the village and came close to the ancient wood Tullynashee which grew on a gentle slope. It was a strange wood as it had the power to change: a path could disappear, a new glade open up, rare flowers and fungi could be found. Most of the inhabitants avoided the wood and said that people had gone in and never returned, but the three children loved Tullynashee and explored it as far as they were able to. They found a badger's set, played hide and seek with tame squirrels, watched birds hatch out of tiny eggs, picked bluebells or St John's wort or collected pine cones for the fire. They kept their voices low and never broke branches, all around them they felt the good will of unseen beings when they found the bright feather of a kingfisher in their path or ripe strawberries and mushrooms to take home.

Tullynashee had no owner though every other piece of land used to belong to a lord or rich farmer.

Pat suggested that they should ask Handy Andy, the joiner, what the name meant, as he was wise and very old. 'Tullynashee means fairy wood and it belongs to those who inhabited Ireland long before Kilcormac was built or a field had been ploughed. It renews itself and has no need of foresters or wood cutters.' The children were fascinated and wanted to know why those ancient people had not all died long ago. 'Have you never heard of the immortals?' he asked them. 'Do you mean the wee folk?' asked Eileen and quickly looked over her shoulder, for the wood was close by. 'The very same, but you better call them the Good People.' Handy Andy looked up from his carpenter's bench where he was always busy and his eyes twinkled. In a strange voice he began to sing:

Handy Andy lives alone in a house that's neither of stick or stone;
Himself and his cat and his speckledy hen, they're living together since dear knows when.

'Are you really so very old?' asked Eileen, but he sang on:

The eagle that flies over Knocknashee is neither as old nor as young as me;
The salmon that sleeps in Owenavoe, I saw his coming, I'll see him go.

'That's a queer song,' said Jimmy. 'I like it but I don't know what it means.' 'Never mind what it means as long as you like it. If you don't like poetry unless you understand the meaning of it, you may leave well alone; it's not for you.'

He stooped to stroke his great orange cat, which was rubbing against his legs. 'Well, is that yourself, Katty Beg? And what have you done with Blatherumskite?' The cat looked up into his face and mewed and at the same time a grey speckledy hen flew in at the door and settled on Andy's shoulder. Andy laid down his hammer and began to unfasten his apron. Looking at the children he sang:

When the cat and the hen come in together
The children should look for a change in the weather;
When Katty comes in with Blatherumskite,
It's time for children to say good night.

Indeed, a fine rain was falling and they took the hint and ran off home. They ran through the evening light with the strange songs ringing in their ears and even in their dreams they heard the voice of Handy Andy echoing.

A few days later the three children were on their way out of the village when they heard a wailing and lamenting coming from a little tumbled down house that stood back from the road. 'Och, och, I am murdered!' screamed the voice. Out of the bothy ran an old woman and behind her, with a broomstick in her hand, came another woman, tall and red-faced, shouting threats and curses. When she saw the children she stopped and turned back to the cottage. The poor victim sobbed, trying to smooth her straggling grey hair with a trembling hand. 'Och, children dear, it's well for me ye came along the road, she'll have me kilt entirely. Och anee, anee, what'll I do? What will I do at all?' 'Wasn't that Ann Foley? Do you live with her? We have never seen you before...' the children asked, full of pity and concern. 'Big Ann Foley she is indeed, and sure where else could I live since I have no roof of my own any longer? She is my cousin, but wicked she is in her moods. She has the life frightened out of me, so she has. Och anee, anee' cried the old body. And when she saw genuine kindness in Eileen, Pat and Jimmy she told her story. When her husband died she had to leave her cottage with vegetables enough for the winter, and strangers moved in to harvest what she had sown. 'Och, it's a hard world when an auld body can't eat her bit in peace.'

She rocked herself backwards and forwards as she sat on a log of fallen trees lying on the grass. 'Is there no other place at all?' asked Eileen. 'No place at all in the wide world, darlin', no place at all. Och, if I had a little house of my own, wouldn't I be a happy woman this day? It's little I need - a bite to eat and a sod of turf for the fire...'. She looked pitiful, the children nearly cried in sympathy.

Pat asked thoughtfully: 'Is there no empty place anywhere? 'Not a one. Mrs Malone would gladly take me in, but she has seven wee ones of her own not to speak of her man. I pay honest for bread and soup but Ann has a temper and she can't control it. I can neither live with her nor without her.'

Looking at the door she whispered: 'Leave me now or it will anger her even more to see me talking with you.'

Sadly the three turned away and made for Handy Andy's house, hoping he had an answer. The old man saw them coming and asked: 'What have you on your mind, you look down in the mouth?' 'We don't know what to do, Andy', said Eileen. 'We met an old woman crying because big Ann Foley torments her and she has nowhere else to live. What can we do to help?' 'Could you not build her a wee house?' asked Pat hopefully. 'No, but I can help you to build one for her.' The children were startled, asking a dozen questions at once. 'Sit down and listen,' he said and they obeyed and sat on the grass. 'There are more ways than one of building a house. Some are made of stone or wood or brick or mud, did you ever hear of a house made of thoughts?'

'Never in my life!' exclaimed Patrick, and the others shook their heads. 'Well, I'll try to explain. Your own parents have built a house of warmth and safety around you by thinking of everything you need and of what you like. Kind thoughts and deeds shelter and protect people and bad temper, greed or hate can make people unhappy or even kill them in the end.'

'Just like Ann Foley could kill the old woman?'

'Yes, one doesn't need to shoot somebody to kill them. Just as you can kill somebody with hate you can build a house with love.' Now the children became quite excited and asked how to set about building such a house. Andy smiled and said: 'Come and follow me so that I can show you what I mean.' Together they walked into Tullynashee and the wood seemed more beautiful than ever. Primroses bordered a path they could not remember ever having seen before, honeysuckle was sending its sweet scent into the air, tall foxgloves grew in ranks and butterflies danced before them. Soon they reached an open glade where Andy pointed to a flat space with rows of large stones laid down in squares or oblongs. The children were puzzled but they walked round the stones and Pat suddenly exclaimed: 'I see, it is the plan for a house!' 'Quite right, these are the foundations well and truly laid.' 'But who did the planning?' asked Jimmy. 'You of course, all three of you.' 'But how? We could not lay these stones without even knowing about it?' Pat stated adamantly.

Andy looked at the three and his eyes were twinkling: 'When you felt sorry for the poor old woman and wanted to help her you started to build her a house of love and compassion.' Eileen was dancing with joy. 'How lovely! And what can we do now to finish it properly?' 'In the same way.

Every good deed or kind thought, any work you do for others without being asked and also any help you offer to man or beast will build this house. But I warn you, if you lose your temper or hurt someone, act selfishly or boast about what you've planned, the building suffers, it may fall down or be destroyed. It is not easy. Do you still wish to go ahead?'

'Yes of course, and can we come every day to look and see how it is growing?'

'You may come as often as you can find the way. I leave you now, for I must feed Katty Beg and Blatherumskite or they'll have my life.'

He left three very thoughtful children behind. Pat asked how the plans could be made real, to think where the kitchen would be and the bedroom. 'But we did not think up these foundations,' said Eileen, 'I believe the house will just grow by itself.' Jimmy said hotly: 'I'm sure Andy laid them and he will just come in secret and build the whole house.' 'But we told him about the old woman only today,' objected Patrick, 'we better find some jobs as he suggested and do the planning in our heads.' 'Oh, how I wish the house was ready,' cried Eileen, 'I want to go straight home and start working, but we must make sure that we find this clearing again and remember the path.'

They discussed jobs and Jimmy declared he would chop wood for the fire and save his father the effort. Eileen noticed the row of washing when she arrived home and for the first time it struck her how many summer dresses and shirts there were, big sheets, towels and trousers. They felt dry and she took them down, folded them as well as she could and then sprinkled them like her mother always did. It kept her busy and gave great satisfaction.

Patrick was walking down the lane when he heard a child crying and soon he discovered a small, very dirty boy in the ditch and helped him out onto firm ground. What a job he had trying to clean the bairn! Then he took him by the hand and walked towards the schoolhouse where he met Mrs Malone in search of her youngest, surrounded by her other children. 'Oh Billy,' she called and he ran into her arms. Pat told her where he had found him and was thanked most warmly. 'Put the kettle on for poor old Kitty Sheehan,' said

Mrs Malone to her eldest daughter. 'Is that the woman who lives with Ann Foley?' asked Patrick. 'Yes, she is an honest soul and worked hard all her life. I wish I could help her more but our house is bursting at the seams.' How Patrick wished to talk about their plans and to comfort Kitty, who had just turned around the corner, yet no words would come. The same happened to Eileen and between them they decided to keep the secret from everybody.

The next day the three children did their chores quickly and made their way to Andy's house where the two animals greeted them loudly; no trace of Andy but cat and hen started with stately dignity along the path to Tullynashee and the children followed them full of expectation. Sure enough the cat led them straight into the clearing while the hen fluttered behind making sure the children were following. Suddenly the house came into view and they gasped with astonishment. The walls were about three feet high, the door frame was in position as were two windowsills. They ran forward and examined the plan of the little cottage. It was easy to make out four rooms, one at each side of the door, two behind at the rear and a hall ran from front to back with doors opening off it.

'Oh, won't old Kitty Sheehan love it! If it goes on growing so quickly she can soon move in.' Pat explained to Jimmy how he had found out the name of the old woman and how they both decided not to tell a soul before the house was finished. 'Rescuing Billy might have helped with the walls just as chopping wood or doing the washing did.' But Jimmy was not certain. 'Andy could have worked through the night I suppose.' A loud miaow from Katty Beg and an angry squawk from Blatherumskite made them jump. 'It looks as if those two understand what we say,' Eileen thought. They saw Andy come towards them with a warm smile. 'How do you like the house you're building?'

'Oh Andy, it is lovely; I wish it was finished and Kitty could move in,' Eileen answered and added: 'If we could only make a garden for her and plant a few flowers.' She had hardly spoken when the soil gave a queer shake and gently moved up in one or two places. The children jumped and Andy just laughed. 'More to come, this looks like the shape of flower beds.' Even Jimmy was impressed and suggested they ought to bring spades next time.

They trooped back with the animals to Andy's cottage and he invited the three children into his comfortable kitchen where the peatfire was burning. They looked curiously around them; the carpenter's shop was on one end, a few armchairs and cupboards at the other. 'What are you making now?' asked Jimmy and inspected the workbench. 'A cradle,' said Andy and began to sing a strange, sleepy air. Soon the children nodded off and began to dream.

> Shoheen, Sholo, and to and fro,
> The mother is singing her child to sleep.
> Shoheen, Sholo, the fire burned low,
> And over the cradle the shadows leap;
> Up the wall and along the rafter,
> One jumps high, and one follows after;
> The room is full of their impish laughter.
> The baby smiles as he falls asleep,
> And over the cradle the shadows creep,
> Singing softly Shoheen, Sholo,
> Follow-my-leader to and fro.

A soft rain fell outside and the children awoke refreshed, and ran home.

When finally the sun showed its face Pat and Eileen's parents drove them into town to buy new shoes and Jim was left on his own. He asked for some cake and tea with sugar which he carried to the bothy to treat Kitty Sheehan to a picnic, but very soon Ann Foley rushed out and threatened him if he didn't stop interfering. When his friends returned he boasted what he had done and without any reason the three quarrelled, called each other names and parted in an angry mood.

A gloriously sunny day followed and, eager to visit the wee house, they made up again and walked to the wood. Tullynashee seemed strangely hostile, the path had disappeared, rocks barred their entry and suddenly Katty Beg turned up with blazing eyes and loud miaows, the hen looked ruffled and annoyed and they both squeezed through a narrow passage. When they followed their arms and legs were scratched by brambles and stung by nettles. They at last saw the glade, but no progress had been made in the house, instead one wall had fallen, window frames were lying on the grass, there was no sign of a garden and an air of dereliction hung over the place.

'Who could have done it? How wicked!' cried Eileen. The animals pointed paw and beak at them and Patrick understood. 'They mean that *we* did it when we were fighting yesterday.' Jim picked up a stone and aimed it at the cat when a loud crack behind him made him pause. The door was swaying on its hinges and fell flat on the ground.
'Poor old Kitty, it's all our fault if she doesn't get her house!' Eileen wept. Deeply ashamed, the children apologised to each other and to the creatures. It looked as if the cat and hen knew what was meant. From behind the house came a pitiful croak and searching among the bushes they found a rook, one wing trailing in a helpless way. Soothingly Pat talked to it and managed to catch the bird before Katty Beg was able to get near it. 'Its wing is broken. Let's take the bird to Andy and he will set it.' It was difficult to carry the rook without getting pecked and to protect it from the cat. A strange noise from the front of the house startled the children: the door lifted itself

and moved back into its proper place. Greatly cheered up they walked into the tree-lined path, no nettles or brambles hindered them this time and the two animals seemed friends again.

Andy set the broken wing with a splint and gave instructions on how to feed the hungry rook with worms and scraps, a job which kept them very busy. Jimmy found an old cage and put the rook into it while they were digging for worms until the garden looked pockmarked and the bird was visibly thriving. They doubled their efforts at home and noticed a new look of gratitude in their parents' eyes. No more skipping jobs, no need to remind them about chopping wood or washing dishes. They discovered how easy any chores became if you did them regularly and willingly.

A bright and sunny day dawned and Eileen's mother packed a picnic basket for the children to take with them. Jimmy joined them with juice and biscuits. To their delight the path was wide open and forget-me-not, meadow-sweet, foxgloves and briar roses flowered in profusion. Thinking of the garden they dug up some wild strawberry plants with their roots and Pat found a young honeysuckle. They arrived at the clearing laden and their hearts rose as they saw the cottage was nearly completed, a thatched roof sat warmly on top and in the garden were beds ready and waiting for the plants. The honeysuckle got a sunny spot near the door and started sending up tiny shoots and flowers. A sweet scent filled the air.

At last they walked inside and found the four rooms complete but empty, no bed, no table, just a wall cupboard and a wide hearth looking as if it badly wanted a fire. 'We need furniture and pots and pans,' said Eileen. 'And firewood' added Pat, 'never mind, let's pretend it's all there and have our tea,' suggested Jimmy who felt hungry.

'Not yet, it's too early. First we should make the kitchen look nice,' Eileen said, and they picked flowers, collected soft green moss, acorn cups and even white mushrooms. The picnic was a success as they shared the food fairly and afterwards tidied the kitchen. They piled sticks against the gable end and left the mushrooms for Kitty to use.

On the village road they came upon poor Kitty Sheehan who was sobbing pitifully. She stopped. 'Oh it's you; I'm moithered with misery, but Mrs Malone is taking me in for the night. Not another hour will I spend under the same roof with Ann Foley. I'd sooner sleep under a tree. Look what she has done to me.' She rolled up her sleeve and showed a cruel bruise on her arm. 'What a shame!' cried Patrick and he looked at the others and raised his eyebrows. They nodded. 'Look, we have found a house for you, it's not quite settled yet but we will come to Mrs Malone's tomorrow at three o'clock and fetch you; will you be there?' 'Och aye, I'll be there and blessings on you if ye can help me.' And she picked up her bundle looking much more cheerful.

The children were deep in thoughts. 'What if there is no bed for her?' Eileen asked. 'Or no water,' added Pat. The bells rang out for evensong and looking at each other they raced towards the church. The door stood open, a few women sat in their pews. An old priest read the text: 'Ask and it will be given, knock and the door will be opened.' Never in their lives had Eileen, Patrick or Jimmy prayed as fervently as on that evening.

Straight after lunch the next day the children ran into the fairy wood carrying a pot and a frying pan they had begged from home. The way seemed so very short and never had the wee house looked more friendly and complete. A pump stood at the very spot where Pat had planned to dig for water; the garden was laid out perfectly and a paved path led to the door. With cries of delight they pushed the door open. The passage was tiled, the walls whitewashed. A table stood in the kitchen and on the mantlepiece a clock was ticking. 'Let's light a fire,' cried Eileen and ran to the little pile of sticks. All the fir cones she had gathered had turned into rich, black turf. While they were blowing at the fire they heard a plop and saw a mushroom hop from the shelf, touch the floor, grow and change its shape into a chair with a padded seat. Five more mushrooms followed and no sooner was the table surrounded by six comfortable chairs when the acorns jumped and alighted on the table, where they became cups and saucers and plates, even a big teapot and sugar bowl appeared. A loud miaow and a squawk at the door and there stood Handy Andy with his companions. 'Well, how do you like it?' he asked smiling, and they all agreed it couldn't be better. 'Come and look at the bedrooms,' he suggested and there they found a big, comfortable bed with a patchwork quilt, a chair and a chest of drawers. They noticed the bare floorboards when suddenly the piece of moss they had gathered came sliding in at the door, stretched itself out, and in a couple of shakes a soft green carpet was laid down.

The second bedroom had two smaller beds and shelves. The last room had a wash basin, towels and a cabinet, everything was perfect. Returning to the kitchen they found pots and pans, a crock full of flour and one of oatmeal, a pound of butter, a dozen eggs and a large jug of milk and fresh scones. 'Can we go and fetch Kitty Sheehan?' asked Patrick eagerly. 'Yes, off with you two boys, Eileen will help me to get the tea ready.'

At Mrs Malone's house the dear old woman was waiting anxiously by the gate while the seven children crowded round her to say goodbye. The boys nearly ran her off her feet but slowed down when they entered Tullynashee which stood in all its summer splendour; on every branch birds were singing, from behind bushes small eyes peeped at them, squirrels climbed high to get a good view and the whole path was bordered with flowers. Then they turned into the glade and beheld the finished house with smoke curling from the chimney and the door opened wide in its welcome. Kitty stood and stared, her breath was taken away and Patrick led her gently into the kitchen where tea was spread out for five guests. Tentatively Kitty touched the chairs, the table, admired the china, looked at the hearth with its fire and sighed deeply. Then her face fell. 'But the rent! Sure I can never pay the rent...' The children looked at Andy who beamed at her: 'No rent to pay, it is all yours and now we hope you will invite us to the party, you are the owner of everything.' Then she wiped away a tear with her apron and set about pouring tea and bustling back and forth, she made toast and saw to the animals, giving milk to Katty Beg and breadcrumbs to Blatherunskite. It was a merry party and it seemed as if the whole glade rejoiced with them. 'Come and see the other rooms,' Jimmy said when he had polished off the last scone. Kitty stood up eagerly. 'I've brought my bundle and would not mind sleeping here on the kitchen floor. This house is even better than my old cottage.' 'You haven't seen the rest, just look at your bed!' cried Eileen and led the way. Lifting her arms the old woman blessed them all and thanked them for the splendid big bed, the green carpet, for everything. Andy guided her to the second bedroom and her face shone with pleasure. 'Och my, I'll be able to invite Mrs Malone's big girls, Mary and Morag. It is awfully cramped in their house.' 'Do you want my old spinning wheel, Kitty?' asked Andy and she smiled dreamily. 'Think ye could spare it? And me old body teaching the girls how to spin. There will be life in this house yet.' After admiring the washroom she looked up at Andy: 'This is a house of safety, no harm will come to anyone under this roof.' 'The house rests on a foundation of pity and compassion, the roof is raised from love and every stone came out of a good and selfless deed.' Then Andy turned to the children and called: 'Fetch more firewood', and after they had run outside Kitty asked: 'How on earth could mere children build such a perfect wee house?' '**Only** children could do it. They believe, and it is faith that fashioned your home. The thousands of beings in Tullynashee are hungry for love and faith. How different the world would be if all humans had love and faith. Doubt destroys and hinders, but this is the last fairy wood in Ireland; from all over Europe the gnomes and elves came with their helpers in air, water and fire to us here. The mind of people grows darker but you remained a child, Kitty, and you will lack nothing. The wealth of the Good People is inexhaustible.'

The house that is built by love and pity is safer than one that is walled around,
Whether in field or in busy city, there will be plenty and peace be found:
Who lives in it lies down to rest with an easy heart and a carefree breast.

Piling the wood next to the hearth the three children heard the song and quietly they wished Kitty Sheehan farewell. They felt richly blessed.

5. The Heather Princess

Far away and long ago, at a time when kings and queens ruled, there was a realm in the Highlands of Scotland in a hidden valley where a river leapt over big boulders and formed a beautiful loch. There a King had built a fine castle from red sandstone where he lived with the queen and his young daughter Fiona. He was respected for his just and fair rule, he was loved for his generosity and kindness, and his people prospered.

On one occasion when the King had to undertake a long journey the valuable treasure of gold and jewellery had been stolen and no trace of the thief could be discovered. But in spite of the loss he felt himself blessed because the loyalty of his wife and subjects remained unchanged and little Fiona filled the palace with her laughter. From her earliest days she had a warm affection for all living creatures. When she had been given a white kitten, and later two white doves, she gave them their food herself and cared for them.

One early spring morning Hamish, the old shepherd, took a motherless lamb to Fiona which she brought up. Soon it followed her on her walks and later her dresses were made of its pure white wool. Her happiness was complete when the king gave her a pony as white as snow and every day she rode around the loch and into the hills, visiting Hamish and his herd, or the families of farmers where she knew every child that was born.

Yet suddenly a shadow fell on the valley and all its inhabitants because more and more sheep disappeared and Hamish himself could not be traced, although a juniper tree grew on the very spot where he had last been seen. For days the young shepherd boy Gavin searched high and low, he walked to the very border where heather and moor formed a paradise for all wild creatures and there he too vanished. The king sent out his soldiers but all they found was a slender birch tree where no such tree had grown before. The King called his daughter and spoke: 'My child, you can no longer roam freely as before nor ride out alone. There is danger in the hills.' And she promised.

Looking longingly to the wild moor one day she noticed a stranger on a dark horse crossing the border. She immediately hurried home where she was greeted by her cat and her lamb. 'Oh, my poor pets, come to the stable and I will feed you,' she cried. As she was busy with milk and hay the doves came too, demanding corn, and soon Fiona forgot the stranger. Contentedly she sat down and cuddled the creatures, which were more like brothers and sisters to the only child. In the meantime the stranger had reached the Palace gate and was greeted respectfully by the guards who led him to the king.

'Welcome, Prince Alastair, heir to my neighbour, come and meet the Queen. I held you in my arms when you were baptised and I have been looking forward to your visit as a young man.' Prince Alastair bowed and took three gifts from his saddle bag. 'Here is a warm rug made from the fur of the first bear I shot, some mead made with pure heather honey, and a small toy, a sailing boat I carved from the antlers of a stag.' His eyes searched the room and the King laughed: 'If you are looking for our Fiona you will have to search the stables, my Prince. Come with me.'

He led the way into the courtyard where a beautiful picture met their eyes. Fiona was sitting in the sunshine fast asleep with a white cat at her feet and a lamb munching hay at her side, while two white doves perched above. Alastair held his breath, never in his life had he seen anything as peaceful and bonny. The white pony came over to wake the Princess and she rubbed her eyes. 'You must be the stranger I saw on the moor. Oh how I wish I was allowed to ride up there again.' Her father introduced the visitor and Alastair gave her the carved sailing boat as a gift made by his own hands. 'Oh thank you, it is more beautiful than any of the treasures my father lost.' Then the King explained how the treasure had been stolen, how the two shepherds vanished after many sheep had disappeared and why Fiona was forbidden to ride out alone. 'Please father, let Alastair come with me. I want to find out where the larks hide their nests and surely I will be safe with the Prince.' 'You will have to ride out before dawn and, if you promise never to let Fiona out of your sight, you have my permission to search for the larks' nests with her tomorrow,' said the King.

It was a glorious morning and the two rode out accompanied by the dawn chorus of numerous birds. 'There is one sure way of discovering the nest of a lark. Lie down among the heather and watch from where they rise. This hollow is a good place. I'll see to the horses.' While Alastair tethered the animals he disturbed a lark and lo, in front of his feet lay a nest with tiny, round eggs.
'Oh look Fiona, I found one for you!' he cried but there was no answer. He looked back and there was nobody; he ran to the little hollow where he had told her to lie down, but it was empty. Lifting his eyes till he could scan the horizon he realised he was alone, except for an old juniper tree and a young birch growing near the heather. Alas, not quite alone. From nowhere an ugly witch appeared with a crooked staff and she mocked him: 'Your little bird is mine. Search as long as you will for the princess, you will never see her again.' Then she stamped her foot and disappeared without a trace. In hopeless despair Alastair roamed the wilderness till finally he rode back to the palace, leading the pony. It was a bitter confession to make, he blamed himself and when the King saw his despair he led the prince into the chapel and together they prayed for Fiona's return.

'One ray of hope is the fact that you have seen the witch whose existence had been hidden from us all these years. I will send out the soldiers and smoke her out of her lair, but you must rest and eat, my son, you are exhausted.'

The Prince took the horses to the stable where the animals surrounded him and it seemed to him as if they knew what had happened. As he fed the pony, lamb and kitten, the doves demanded grain and only when they had their share he returned to the King and Queen. With outstretched hands the Queen greeted him: 'Keep hope alive, Alastair, this very morning a voice spoke to me and said that before the candles have burnt down in the chapel a greater treasure will be returned to us than the one the kingdom has lost, and is Fiona not our greatest treasure?'

The soldiers came back defeated in their search by darkness. Alastair saddled his horse in grey dawn. The white pony nudged him, the doves cooed and the lamb followed him out of the yard while the cat jumped onto the saddle. 'Come with me and find Fiona,' he called and the strange procession set off.

Soon they reached the little hollow where he had last seen Fiona. The doves flew overhead, the pony followed closely, the cat jumped from her perch and the lamb came running along. It seemed as if they knew something and, while Alastair was straining his eyes to gaze far out over the purple heather the, animals formed a perfect circle. At this moment the sun rose and illuminated the moor, every dew drop sparkled, even the ancient juniper tree waved its branches as the animals broke into a chorus. The prince slipped from the saddle to see what they were all gazing at with such excitement. There in the centre grew a fine clump of snow-white heather, opening its delicate flowers to drink in the dew and sun. His heart told him that this was the lost princess.

A cloud slid over the sun, a cold wind arose and a nasty voice cut through his reverie: 'Haha, those dumb beasts have more sense than you have and all the king's soldiers together. See what a fool you have been! I will win power over all of you and you shall be my servant.' The witch stood with the crooked staff and pointed to a trapdoor: 'That is *my* palace!' A steep stair led into darkness, a stench filled the air. 'You may kiss your sweetheart for the last time.' The moment Alastair bent down to kiss the sweet white heather the pony neighed, the cat miaowed, the lamb bleated and he swung around to see how the witch raise her staff menacingly towards him. He whipped it out of her hand and shouted: 'Turn to stone!' And a black stone fell to the ground.

Sunshine returned to the glen, a peel of laughter rose from the little hollow as Fiona awoke from the spell and saw her animals with surprise: 'My friends, how did you come to be here?' Before anybody could answer, the juniper tree shook and out stepped Hamish, the shepherd, rubbing his eyes as if after a long sleep. The young birch released a boy who was greeted as Gavin, lost for many months. Joy filled the morning and Alastair told how all of them had been saved by the wise animals. 'Let us now have a look at the witch's palace where I was meant to slave my life away.' Alastair climbed down the steps and called: 'Hamish, come and help me.' When his eyes had adjusted to the gloom Hamish saw masses of bones. 'My poor sheep will not return to life.. but what's that box you have there?' 'It looks like an old treasure chest, beautifully carved, only that it is covered in filth.' Alastair could hardly lift it and Gavin came down as well to help. The shepherd and Gavin heaved, and together they carried a heavy wooden box up the steps. Fiona came closer to look. The lid was carved with an intricate pattern, the lock was open. Inside were the lost treasures of the kingdom, stolen so long ago. Fiona sent her two doves to the palace to bring the good news and while the black horse carried the treasure, guided by Alastair, the princess rode on her pony accompanied by Hamish, Gavin and the rest of her pets. From every farm the people emerged and when the procession could be seen from the palace the bells began to ring out over the valley.

Deeply moved, the King and Queen greeted Fiona and when they saw the treasure the King proclaimed a great festival should be held, all work was to cease to celebrate the liberation of the Princess Fiona, of Hamish and Gavin, and the return of the gold. He praised Alastair who had overcome the evil old witch and found the treasure. 'Do not thank me. If it had not been for these faithful animals I would now either slave in the dungeon or lie under a spell myself.'

The jubilation knew no end, music was played, the children danced and long tables were set up for a feast the like of which nobody had ever seen before. From this day onwards white heather has been found in the glen as proof that this story is true. Go and look for yourself!

6. The Bride from the Sea

Donald was a strong man; he had built his house with his own two hands, thatched the roof with straw and tied it down with stones so that no storm could shift it. His fields carried a good harvest year by year, and he owned a boat for fishing. Many a girl fancied him but he was content to live alone with Coolie the dog, until one day all that changed.

It was spring and Donald had gone to the beach with a hand cart to fetch seaweed for the lazy-beds, as he used to do every year to make the soil more fertile. He had just filled the cart and was busy turning it round when he heard a delicate song from the next bay. Quietly he crept over the sand and beyond the cliffs he beheld three lovely figures sitting on a rock singing. One of the maidens had black hair, one red, but the third was fair and her hair shone lovelier than pure gold. Undetected, he crept closer and just when he could have touched her his dog barked and the three girls leapt into the sea, and all he could make out were three seals' heads bobbing in the water. He was vexed indeed and pulling his cart homewards he met old Kieran who called out to him: 'What's up? You look as if you have seen a ghost.' Then Donald told him all that had happened and asked: 'How will I ever see the girls again? Without the blonde one my life seems meaningless and empty. Who could she be?' 'What will you give me if I tell you the answer?' said Kieran. 'I'll give you this whole load of seaweed.' 'Ah, if you would also spread it over my piece of land I'll solve the riddle.'

Donald obliged and soon the load of green manure was spread out and old Kieran lit his pipe and said: 'Every year after the great spring tide the three daughters of the King of the Sea come to our strand to sing their songs. Each of them has a grey seal skin rolled up, lying on the rock. If you succeed in getting hold of her skin the girl has got to follow you and stay with you, but take great care that the skin never dries out or she will die. If she discovers where her skin is she will disappear into the sea forever.' 'Thank you for your advice, I will remember it well,' answered Donald; and from that day on he worked twice as hard. He whitewashed the cottage, he built a splendid double bed and a chest of drawers. He planted a rosebush next to the front door, enlarged his acre of land, planted more vegetables and finally he went into town to buy a large soft shawl and a fine dress.

Spring came and with it the great tide. Carefully Donald locked Coolie in before he went down to the sea where he waited patiently, well hidden behind rocks. He watched the three seals change into maidens, he listened to the lilting songs and again it was the golden-haired girl that cast her spell on him. He crept closer, and grabbed her skin when two of the girls jumped into the sea. The third one wept and pleaded with him, but he threw the woollen shawl over her and led her to his house. A glowing peatfire burned in the hearth and a dress was waiting for her. The smell of a delicious stew filled the room.

Donald married his beautiful bride from the sea and he read every wish from her lips, but Mari never smiled. She was a good wife, and, when after a year a son was born, Donald saw a tender smile on her face. Four more children followed and warm life filled the house. It was Jamie, the fifth, whom she loved most and he followed her everywhere and refused to travel into town with the others, but rather stayed with Mari. Yet it was Jamie who brought the happiness to a sudden end.

It was spring again, and one early morning when Jamie woke up he heard his father creep down the stairs. Curiosity made him follow quietly out of the door and round to the back. Soft-footed he turned the corner and saw how his father lifted a stone from the wall, pulled out a grey skin and spread it on the ground in order to rub some grease into it. Unseen the boy returned to his warm bed and forgot all about it. After his brothers and sisters had gone to the field he helped at home and, while Mari was kneading the dough, he asked innocently: 'Why does father hide an old skin in the wall outside?' Mari stared at him, her body rigid, and asked: 'Where is this place, Jamie? Show it to me at once.' Struck dumb by the change in his mother's voice, little Jamie walked in silence to the back of the house and pointed to a stone in the wall that was loose. Within seconds Mari had pulled it out and she hugged the smooth and supple skin to her heart. Then she turned to the boy and cried: 'Oh my darling, my precious child, a thousand thanks to you. Deep under the sea I have another family. For many years my five other children have missed me and I have missed them. Tell your father that I thank him for his love and care. I will be close to him even if he cannot see me. Greet your brothers and sisters from me, their lives will be blessed.' She hugged Jamie once more.

Turning to the sea he heard her laugh, a wild and free laugh that rang out over the water, and she ran into the waves until only the small, grey head of a seal could be seen.

Tired and spent by the day's work, Donald returned from the field with his children. There was no food prepared, the bread had not been baked, the fire was almost extinguished. Jamie was sobbing his heart out and it took time to calm him sufficiently so he could speak. He gave the message and described what had happened. Then he stood up and looking at his father he said: 'And she laughed out loud, our mother was laughing for the first time.'

From this day on Donald left the work on the land to the older children. He himself sailed out to sea and went fishing every day. As if steered by invisible hands he found a rich harvest and his nets were always full. He got good money for his catch on the market and life was better in every way except for the loss of wife and mother.

In the autumn, after all of his neighbours had pulled their boats high onto the sands to save them from winter storms, Donald sailed out into the huge waves of the Atlantic. Giant waves crashed down on his vessel, the mast broke and, when it seemed as if nothing could save him from drowning, two gigantic seals came alongside and kept the boat afloat, steering it back to the land.

Old Kieran found the fisherman unconscious but unhurt near the rock where he had seen his bride for the first time so many years ago. And even today, hundred of years later, those who dwell around the bay speak of Donald and his love, of Mari and her faithfulness.

7. Daughter of the Fairy Queen

Myrna was truly happy in her warm and safe stone house on the south coast of Ireland where land and water penetrate each other intimately and where music and poetry have their home. Kevin, her faithful husband, brought fresh fish from his daily trips and he made sure there was enough peat piled against the wall and plenty of vegetables in the cottage garden. In the evenings Myrna would play the Clarsach and her brown eyes shone with love when Kevin sang the age old-songs in Gaelic.

After the summer had gone Myrna gave birth to a fine boy and the father said proudly: 'He will lack nothing as long as I live.' And he doubled his effort to catch fish, defying the autumn storms, however much his wife begged him to stay at home. After Samhain his empty boat drifted into the bay. Wild were the cries of the seagulls, but wilder those of Myrna in her despair, and if it hadn't been for wee baby Kevin she would have followed her husband into the waves. Her stores ran low, finally there was just enough flour in the larder and oil in the jug to bake one last pancake and she was weeping while she stirred the batter.

She heard knocking at the door but when she opened it there seemed to be nothing but the empty beach. Then she heard a fine voice: 'Look down, it is I, the Queen of the Fairies.' Minute was the green figure on the threshold, yet smaller still the pale and fragile child she held in her arms. Myrna welcomed the guest and led her into the house.
'My daughter is dying, I have no milk to feed her and I beseech you to take her to your breast.'
'How can I fulfil your wish if want lives in my house and I am starving? See, here is the last of the flour, the last drop of oil and tell me what I can do.' With a gesture of

blessing the queen touched every jug and flagon, casket
and crock, chanting a mantram:

Plenty of food,
Plenty of drink,
Fullness of life
For you and your kin.

Invisible hands filled every container in the kitchen, fresh
butter stood on the table with a crusty loaf of bread. The
queen handed her child to Myrna and before she left she
blessed the cradle in which Kevin was fast asleep. 'Wait for
me to return in a year and a day. All will be well,' she said.

Soon the two infants became best friends, both were
thriving and no more want was felt in the cottage. Music
and harp playing, singing and laughing could be heard,
and time flew past till the knock at the door told Myrna
that a year and a day had gone. Proudly she returned the
wee elf, radiant with health, and the queen took her into
her arms. 'Come with me to receive your reward,' she said
and led the way to the steep cliff which surrounded the
lonely bay. Hesitantly Myrna followed with Kevin. The
fairy moved a blanket of hanging heather aside and
revealed an open gate which led into a bright realm of
light where trees were laden with fruit, and honey filled
the air with sweet scent. Tiny creatures flew around them,
a long table was laid for a feast and the queen guided
Myrna to the place of honour and sat her down on a chair
adorned with garlands of flowers. Never had she dreamt of
such delicious food, her glass was filled with elderberry
wine and there was great rejoicing. She forgot to be shy
and enjoyed the company of creatures never seen before
by human eyes. Kevin stuffed himself with honey cakes
and she felt proud of the queen's daughter who was the
centre of attention. When she could eat no more the queen
showed her two sacks made of silk. 'Choose your reward,

Myrna, saviour of my child. One sack filled with pearls and precious stones, the other with seeds and herbs to cure any illness under the sun. Choose wisely for you will grow very old.' Myrna first felt the heavy sack, then the light one and answered: 'Please give me the seeds and herbs, but also the wisdom to use them well.' 'Well chosen! May your hands be blessed and your mind enlightened.' The Queen of Fairyland clapped her hands and suddenly Myrna found herself in front of her own fisher-house with Kevin clutching her hand. In her skirt lay the silken sack filled with numerous seeds and dried herbs.

Never again did Myrna lack anything. Her garden was filled with aromatic herbs and people came from far and wide, by boat or on foot, to seek her advice and find healing. She never found the door behind the blanket of heather again and never saw her benefactress; but, whenever she wanted advice as to which herb to use, all she needed to do was to close her eyes and send a prayer to Mary, the mother of the King of Kings, and an answer was granted. From her small garden radiated health and healing to young and old.

8. The Towering Angel

This is a true story and it took place in one of the health resorts in the South of Ireland in the beginning of this century. I heard it from a lady who herself was old while I was still young, but it has remained with me ever since. In order that you may believe it, I let her speak as she spoke to me all those years ago:

'They were hard times after the first World War and I had been very ill when my doctor advised me to move close to the sea in the south, where palm trees grow and the winters are mild, to spend six months resting. I had no savings and it meant selling my scant possessions, packing a suitcase and travelling to one of the cheaper holiday towns at the coast. It was chilly, most of the summer visitors had gone and I dragged the heavy case along the promenade, feeling faint with hunger. My heart sank when I saw the grand hotels, the ugly guesthouses, and I felt despair at finding a warm and homely place to stay. The thought of inquisitive landladies, dull rooms and indifferent food depressed me. It was a long way to the cheaper end of the promenade and what I saw there promised neither warmth nor hospitality.

I put my case down, took a deep breath and with all the strength of soul I prayed to my guardian angel, as I was wont to do as a child. A quickening vitality streamed through my body, the burden seemed lighter and I sensed a footstep next to mine, but there was nobody to be seen anywhere. "Look up," whispered an inner voice and gradually a figure condensed to visibility, a towering angel of great beauty who had taken on the weight of my case without even touching it. As if it was a matter of course he began to speak to me, telling me of a good hostel nearby which could be trusted.

We left the promenade and turned into a quiet lane where I looked fully into the radiant figure of my spiritual companion with his strong face before he gestured towards a small, modest cottage and dissolved. How long I stood there I cannot remember; I was filled with such an incredible bliss that time did not matter anymore.

The door opened and a pleasant-looking lady welcomed me in and offered me tea. I introduced myself. She took the suitcase, led me into a comfortable sitting-room where a bright fire was burning in the grate and she made fresh tea. Then I told this stranger my innermost thoughts, and explained the circumstances of my illness. Conventional restraint vanished, I felt confident that truth and only truth mattered and, as the words tumbled out, I felt liberated from the shame of my poverty and my sickness. It was like a physical tonic. My hostess didn't interrupt me and showed no surprise or impatience. Calm, but with an undisguised joy, she looked at me from her warm, dark brown eyes, and filled the cup a second and a third time till all my problems lay open before her. Then something unexpected happened: tears began to stream from her eyes, glad tears, tears of gratitude as she explained to me. The night before she had sat down with her ledger to add up her assets and had come to the conclusion that, unless she found a lodger for the winter, she would have to sell her father's house which she loved more that anything. In her great distress she had gone down to the sea at sunset and sent her supplication into the wind. All her pain and trouble were poured out in prayer, facing the sun and the sea. This morning she had woken up with the certainty that her prayer would be answered. She had gone to air the guest room and spread fresh linen on the bed, everything was ready for her visitor. The sum I had mentioned would be sufficient to live simply, she knew a great deal about nursing and my symptoms did not frighten or worry her.

The winter became a wonderfully rich and rewarding time of friendship and sharing. My health was restored and she taught me the blessing of open confidence and truthfulness, curing me of all traces of conventional habits. She spoke of the Lady Poverty like St. Francis had done and how much she had learnt from her. I enjoyed her cooking and even nettle soup tasted agreeable. During the long winter evenings she taught me how to make a new dress out of two old ones and how to keep a peat fire burning through the night. Looking back I am still filled with gratitude and I know I gained back more than my physical health.'

9. The Empty Cradle

In the life of the hill farmer MacNamara the most important creature was his cow Daisy. Her existence marked the difference between him and the other small crofters who had to eke out a living with sheep only. Every day he measured the creamy milk Daisy produced before any other job on the farm began. His cheeses were made by his wife and fetched good prices in the market town.

It had not always been like this. When he courted bonny Lily and took her home his life had centred round the coming heir who was to carry his name; then he had spent every evening carving a most intricate Celtic pattern on the cradle he had built himself while Lily filled a chest with dainty jackets and shawls, vests and bonnets. But after a stillborn baby wrecked his hopes he looked at the cradle with resentment and he rather concentrated on Daisy and her virtues. Lily never gave up hope though, spinning ever finer woollen threads to knit and weave for a miracle child so desperately prayed for every day and night.

Another autumn came, the harvest had been safely brought in and Daisy took up residence in the clean stable, filled with the scent of fresh hay. But one morning MacNamara came into the kitchen with a curse on his lips. 'Somebody has secretly milked my cow,' and he showed Lily the bucket which was not as full as usual. 'Who dares to steal my milk? I will teach the thief a lesson he will not forget.' And he placed his gun near the bedpost, determined to watch the next night. But sleep overcame him and it was Lily who heard the stable door creaking at 4 o'clock before dawn. Quietly she slipped out of bed and watched from the window as a slim female figure crept stealthily out of the stable and across the yard to disappear in the direction of the forest. Lily did not dare waken her husband, and his anger at the missing milk next morning grew into a fury.

'I will take the chain from the watchdog tonight! Boris will catch the thief no doubt,' he yelled, but Lily's heart beat anxiously. Still, it was she who slept and only when her husband jumped to the window with a gun in his hand did she wake up. 'Don't shoot!' she cried and ran to his side, just in time to see the same figure glide across the yard and it seemed as if it was almost transparent and unearthly. The dog stood rooted to the ground, his fur bristling.

MacNamara sat down heavily, pulled on his boots, took the gun and made for the door. 'Wait, please,' Lily implored him, 'Let me make you some coffee, it is a cold night.' He nodded, fetched some kindling and blew into the ashes. The hot drink revived their spirits and they were able to speak about what they had seen. A pale dawn promised another day and the farmer said very quietly: 'Perhaps somebody needs Daisy's milk more than we do.' Surprised and comforted, Lily placed her hand into his and spoke encouragingly: 'Let us go together and look.'

There was no trace of footsteps on the wet loam, no sign of a human being. Where the figure had vanished stood a crippled old oak. Cautiously they walked closer and in the first rays of the sun they saw something rosy, something that was moving. It was a small baby, a few days old, wrapped in a white shawl. Lily trembled as she took this gift of God to her breast and MacNamara embraced the two with both his arms and gazed at the child. He saw a drop of milk on his lips: Daisy's milk!

With infinite tenderness the parents bedded the little boy into the waiting cradle and he opened his blue eyes wide and looked up at them. Then Lily took a candle and lit it in front of a picture of Mother Mary to thank her for the miracle.

On his next visit to the market MacNamara heard how in the last bothy at the top of the valley the eldest daughter had ran away when she could no longer hide her swelling belly. They had found her body but no trace of the child. The family belonged to the poorest of the poor and declared themselves relieved that they were not forced to feed another mouth. 'When did that happen?' asked the farmer. 'When you took your cow into the stable, around Michaelmas,' was the answer. With a deep sigh of relief MacNamara thanked the speaker and went home satisfied that nobody would claim their son. 'And we will call him Michael', he added and took his wife into his arms.

10.   The Foolish Potter

Once upon a time there lived a man whose name has been forgotten because everybody called him the Foolish Potter. He did not mind, he was a kind and gentle man and his eyes were as blue as the sea in summer and had a far-away look; his face was full of smiles. He had a curly beard and strong hands and he lived with his black cat, Nero, behind a farm. All he possessed was a potter's wheel, a stove to fire the crockery, and brushes and pots of paints in all the colours of the rainbow. Though he was poor, Nero never missed a meal and Nero kept the barn and stable free from mice.

A widow lived on the farm with her seven sons whom she brought up as well as she could. Every night she would light a candle for her husband. In its light she felt his presence and she would turn to him with any question. One evening she folded her hands and said: 'The boys are getting too big for me to handle, please send me a helper!' She had fallen asleep full of trust, thinking of each of her sons and his particular need.

Not long afterwards the young potter had walked down into the valley and stopped at her door, asking for a glass of buttermilk. She invited him in for a good meal and he spoke of his wish to build up a pottery. The widow looked into his innocent eyes and at his strong hands and she offered him the shed behind the courtyard. Hardly had he set up his workshop when the boys crowded around him and asked a hundred questions. Then the widow knew her prayer had been answered. Gratefully she watched the kind of teaching he offered while his hands were busy shaping plates and pots. He spoke of each plant in the meadows, each creature in wood or field as if he had been present when God had made them all. He taught reverence for life and compassion

71

to all beings. But his first question was always: 'Have you done your chores?' Only when the cow was milked, the eggs gathered, the firewood chopped and water pumped for the kitchen did the stories flow.

The potter knew many verses which he recited till all seven boys were able to repeat them:

Bless, O God, my little cow,
Bless, O God, my desire,
Bless Thou my partnership,
And the milking of my hands.

Bless, O God, each teat,
Bless, O God, each finger,
Bless Thou each drop
That goes into my pitcher.

Give the milk
Get a reward,
Bannock of quern,
Sap of ale-wort,
Wine of chalice,
Honey and the wealth of the milk,
My treasure.

Give the milk,
Get a reward,
Grasses of plain,
Milk of the field,
Ale of the malt,
Music of the lyre,
My treasure.

Give the milk
And have the blessing
Of the King of the earth,

The King of the sea,
The King of the angels,
The King of the City,
My treasure.

He had verses for collecting eggs, for the sowing of seeds and for cutting the hay. When every job was done new stories would follow about giants and gnomes, enchanted princes and knights of the Holy Grail.

On market days he would load a wheelbarrow with his wares and everybody would crowd around him but he did not sell very much. The problem was that he sold no plain dishes. There were mugs with toes sticking out, jugs with handles shaped like a maiden, peacocks painted on plates and bears on bowls, delicate butterflies on cream jugs and kingfishers on vases. They were beautiful and he offered them cheaply but people had always eaten from thick brown earthenware dishes with never as much as a flower on it. Luckily there were always children who begged for pretty plates and he made a splendid trade in gnomes, two to a penny.

The widow was a sensible woman and advised him to produce what folk wanted, and, because he respected her, he made dozens of plain pieces of crockery but his face grew sad, no songs came from his lips and no stories either. As soon as he had money in his pocket he bought a pretty apron for the widow and sugar almonds for the boys, out came the paintbrushes and an exquisite pattern graced the next teapot. By his happy voice the boys would know that soon a new seam of stories would be worked for them, recalling the history of the world or great deeds of men and saints.

In gratitude the boys did everything for him without being asked: filled Nero's saucer with milk, fed the ever-hungry furnace with wood, and drew water. Never a day passed without some lessons, yet any teacher would have shaken his head if he had listened. When slugs threatened the cabbage he told the boys to sprinkle bran under the larger leaves and lo, the slugs came to eat the bait and next morning it was easy to destroy them. Before carrot seeds were sown the potter clipped the boys' hair, collected the stubble and mixed the seeds with them: no pest attacked the carrots! When a plague of moles ruined the meadow he taught the children to make paper windmills, stick them into each molehill and soon the furry dwellers left of their own free will. No wonder the people called him a Foolish Potter when they heard of such teachings.

However, the farm flourished, no beast fell ill, the harvest was rich, the bees doubled their store of honey after wild parsnips, melissa, borage and hyssop had been planted in the garden, and the skep had a branch of juniper tree hanging inside. Hedgehogs were fed and encouraged to feed on grubs, a toad lived under a pot near the pump, and before a calf was due the potter mixed cider vinegar under the fodder to ensure a healthy birth.

It was a fertile valley, many a journeyman walked through it and when they heard stories of the Foolish Potter they would come and look at the piles of strange objects, handle the clay, marvel at the colours and he would give away samples; but not one of the passing potters could ever copy the texture of his wares. 'Move into town, you can make a fortune!' they advised, but he smiled and answered: 'I have seven reasons to stay where I am.'

The autumn brought a profusion of berries, and our friend took the boys picking brambles and crab-apples, but he warned that a cold winter would follow. The widow requested a tiled stove and with great enthusiasm he created a masterpiece: on each tile a scene from the creation of the world was painted, with Adam and Eve, the wicked snake, all the animals of Noah's Ark and many more. Soon he discovered Gavin, the second son, at his elbow, tracing figures, learning to draw, and the potter promised to teach him the trade. The widow was glad and within a short time the making of plain pots and plates could be left to him. In every spare moment Gavin practised painting. He was told to watch a cock stride across the yard, tail feathers shining, the throat working up and down before crowing and only when Gavin had made himself creep inside the cock, think and feel like a cock who is king of his roost, only then to dip his brush into the paint. Gavin watched a kingfisher skim the water, a swallow build its nest, an owl in flight at dusk. He then filled a sketchbook for his master to judge.

Tossing a lump of clay to Gavin the potter encouraged him to copy Nero licking his haunches, arching his back or limply curled up in sleep. Soon the young apprentice created his own style and that was joy for his teacher. One day Gavin asked: 'Tell me the secret of your work. Nobody else has the smooth finish, the brilliant colours; it's like magic.' The Foolish Potter lit his pipe and replied: 'Yes it is magic indeed and I wonder if you'll believe my story. It is time you knew my secret.'

They sat alone by the newly-completed tiled stove, apples were roasting and Nero purred contentedly. 'My master was a hard man and strict with us, he beat us if we ruined a piece and forced us apprentices to repeat the same form over and over until our fingers were stiff; I used every chance to get into the open, fetch fresh clay or gather wood. There was plenty of coarse clay and it took little time to fill the buckets. Then I would run to a little knoll, eat my bread and cheese, whistle a tune and, before I left, leave the best morsels for the fairies. Oh, how I had to run back to avoid a beating! One balmy evening I wandered further, past the knoll into a moor, with my bare feet. Suddenly I took fright, the swamp was dangerous, people had disappeared without a trace and far and wide nobody was abroad. With all my strength I prayed for help. A tiny voice answered. I saw nobody but felt a tug at my trousers. There below me stood a wee manikin with a green cap and rusty red waistcoat. "My child, fear not, I'll guide you through the moor," said he, and when he saw my astonished face he added: "You are expected." The gnome looked ancient and yet there was laughter in his eyes and I trusted him, pulled my feet from the wet quicksand and followed him from one dry tussock to the next till we reached a juniper tree on firm ground. "My master has sent for you to thank you for the gifts. Though we are never in want of food what we do need is bread given with love, for otherwise we lack joy and festive fun. A few crumbs are enough for us." With these words my guide steered me through a thick hawthorn hedge without a scratch, it was as if the thorns pulled back. On the other side a beautiful sight met my eyes: a wide meadow within a sheltering ring of trees, a stage set for dancing, and thousands of tiny creatures celebrating a festival of music. Flutes and harps, bells and strings played in sweet harmony. Elves and dwarfs, butterflies and dragonflies, bumble bees and beetles crowded around a table filled with dishes more delicate than you have ever tasted. I joined in, I danced and ate my fill of mushrooms, nuts and honey cakes till in my soul a picture rose of Mary walking through the thorny wood, finding a stable in the darkest winter night, warmed by the breath of ox and ass, giving birth to Jesus, visited by shepherds, surrounded by the song and music of angels...the moon rose, it was so still as they all listened to the one story they longed to hear.

In my pocket I carried as always a silver beaker which I gave to my guardian and as it went from hand to hand, the gnomes admired it greatly. This I knew well: no mortal may visit the Little People without a gift. They promised to show me a hidden place for finer clay if I cared to return at the next full moon.

I walked back across the swamp like a sleepwalker under the safe guidance of my small friend and from that day on I thought of nothing else. Neither a scolding by the master nor any mocking from the other fellows ruffled my spirit: I counted the days to the next full moon. With every pocket stuffed full of candy and fresh hazelnuts I crossed the moor to find the festivities in full swing, and I joined in wholeheartedly. After the dancing I cracked the nuts and earned loud praise. "Nuts make you wise!" the gnomes told me, and wise indeed these earth-beings are. At story time I was well prepared, having studied Matthew's account of the noble birth announced by a star, and it became clear how the intimate link between the three kings and the royal child with the star was of great interest to these elemental beings.

As a parting gift a lump of the finest clay was given to me and I promised not to allow anybody to see or touch it, but to work with it in secret. You, Gavin, are the first to hear about it because my friends gave me permission. Never before had I handled such clay; Soft and smooth it was and I fashioned a new beaker with intricate celtic pattern. When I showed it to the gnome he took me to a distant field where a ruined chapel stood. "Eight hundred years ago a monk lived here and sang his prayers four times a day over the land. Later a bell was hung up and chimed morning, noon and night. This field was ploughed and harrowed while the bells were ringing and the holy sound penetrated the very soil. Deep below we felt how the ringing of the bell ploughed into the earth and its harmonies refined the clay. Guard the secret well." Then he warned me never to smoke tobacco, as it would prevent me from seeing the Little People. "Since men began to smoke they have felt cut off from the spirits above and the beings below; many elementals have had to flee. Who knows how long we will be safe in our glade behind the hawthorn hedge? We work in rock and metal, in crystals and roots of trees; Undines live in flowing waters, sylphs in the air, yet far higher beings work through us and we serve them gladly. Take this clay and serve them as we do. Do not work for riches or fame."

Since then many years passed, I finished my apprenticeship and my master used me for difficult tasks, making me produce pieces for which he was well paid; finally the Guild was to examine me at Whitsun. Hoping for the title of a master potter, I worked hard and I won a competition, but before the examination I visited my friends once more and found them in a sombre mood. "The salamander or fire beings have come and complained bitterly how the town stank from pipe smoking, how even women and children chewed tobacco and only a terrible catastrophe would cleanse the city. They gave a warning not to remain within the walls on Whit Sunday; it would be a matter of life and death." Thus spoke my friend the gnome and implored me to obey the warning. What was I to do? Leaving without the certificate the long years of training would be wasted, but I decided to obey.

Early that morning all my fellow journeymen, the potters, weavers, goldsmiths and joiners walked in festive dress to the town hall while I packed my rucksack and made my way to the exit gate. "There goes the Foolish Potter!" they cried, relieved not to have to compete with me. Every house was decorated with green garlands, people were laughing, children playing, a holiday mood embraced all citizens and who was I to turn my back on them? My heart was heavy, it was hot, far too hot for this time of year. The narrow lanes were airless and I took a deep breath after leaving the city gate. Following yonder river I reached my fairy knoll and turned around to wave farewell to my home town.

Oh Gavin, as long as I live I will remember the sight: the city was burning! Red flames burst from the town hall, showers of sparks were blown over the roofs, a wind fanned the fire and suddenly all the bells began to toll. The houses burnt like dry cinder, an inferno raged between those old walls, people began streaming out of the gates; tears fell from my eyes. There was nothing I could do to help.

A tug on my trousers made me look down; my wee friend stood below and said to me: "The men caused the fire with their own pipes, it had to happen, but you must follow your path; we will guide you to find good people where you are needed." He gave me a bundle of precious clay. Resolutely I turned my back on the fire and walked on towards the forest above your valley. When I saw the farmhouse here your mother's prayer floated like a cloud above it and my little guide confirmed my own choice. The rest you know yourself. My friends have invited you to meet them when more finer clay is needed.'

Deeply moved Gavin nodded: 'I am glad to see the elementals! One question remains though. Why do you etch T.T. only onto your best pieces?' The potter laughed: 'It means Tinkling Tone and we ought to make a set of bells with our finest clay which rings out like the bells of wee fairies.' 'Perhaps my journeyman's piece?' asked Gavin eagerly. 'The clear sound of churchbells penetrated this clay and it will echo back to us into our present time. Yes, try your hand on a range of tintinnabulums or tinkling bells and for you there will be no restrictions, you may become rich and famous.'

Gavin was wise beyond his years and he became a friend of the Little People, respecting their secret. He felt they longed for human friendship and trust, yes *trust* they longed for in a darkening world. He did not disdain the job with ordinary clay for plain dishes, and soon his wares became popular in the village.

Whitsun came in glorious splendour with blue skies and a brilliant sun. A great event was to happen: the Queen wanted to visit the valley. Every house was cleaned and whitewashed, birches planted in pots at front doors, children gathered flowers and lined the road in their Sunday best, the air hummed with excitement, a band was playing. High up at the top of the valley a coach emerged from the wood, pulled by six white horses, a gentle face looking out of the window.

The seven sons wore fresh white shirts, their hair brushed, their knees scrubbed; even the potter displayed a new suit and the widow wore a silk dress. Trumpeters blew and the coach halted at the farm, the queen stepped out, the boys bowed. 'My good woman, I've been told you raise your sons all alone,' said the Queen. 'I too am on my own; tell me, do you need to use the birch on their backs?' 'Oh, not ever since our potter has taken over their education and I'm no longer alone. When my husband was killed by a falling tree I was often in despair. In prayer I asked him to send a helper and he did.' The Potter bowed. 'Tell me, what is your secret? I have to be just and do not wish to be harsh,' said the Queen. 'Our schoolroom is the pottery where the pupils can watch the creation of beautiful things and while they watch I tell them stories of Kings and Queens; of how good wins over evil and how a wicked witch will want to be burnt in order to be transformed.' His eyes twinkled and he added: 'And my pupils teach me more that I could ever teach them.'

The Queen was delighted and wanted to see the pottery. She was utterly amazed at the fine china, the elegant tea-sets, artistic vases and plates, the masterly workmanship. 'May I purchase your wares?' she asked and he nodded. Great boxes were filled while the widow invited the Queen to enter the house where a table was laid. In the room stood the tiled stove with its splendid illustrations of the creation story and looking at the pictures she demanded that the potter should follow her to the castle and become the court's Master of Ceramic.

'O no,' he exclaimed, 'thank you for the offer but I have seven reasons to stay here,' and he pointed to the children. Then the Queen pulled out a purse, and gave it to him with the words: 'Here is some gold for the goods I have bought now; and for next winter I order you to build a tiled stove for the castle with pictures of the New Testament. I honour your reason for remaining here and I'm sure the tiles can be fashioned in this place meanwhile.' The purse was heavy and the potter wanted to return it to the Queen. 'Your Majesty, this gold I cannot take as I do not possess a Master's title. It is an honour for me if you accept them as a gift.' He bowed deeply. 'Then give the purse to the good widow. I will send builders to erect a new pottery on the farm if she agrees, a bigger place for training many more apprentices. But tell me where you learnt your trade.' Thus spoke the Queen and when the potter named the city she nodded: 'I heard of the fire, you were lucky to escape the inferno. My own judgement tells me that your work counts among the best I have seen anywhere. A degree will be conferred to you in good time.'

Meanwhile a restless crowd had gathered outside, waiting to greet the Queen. 'What do you call this man?' she asked. Shamefully came the reply: 'The Foolish Potter', and it became a title of praise rather than mockery. Famous the potter became but modest he remained.

11. The Mirror

In the south west of Ireland lies a small village with an open harbour facing the Atlantic and there once lived the beautiful Mrs Sheena Malore with her daughter Isabel, in the house of the restless Brendan, who was well-known in every seaside town but who sat rarely at his own hearth. Sheena was shunned by the villagers. She had come from Dublin and had nothing in common with the other women. She still wore her city clothes, she even went to church with a hat instead of tying a shawl over her head as everybody else did.

Isabel had inherited the beauty of her mother and she was popular with old and young. She did her work well and was quick on her feet, had a kind word for her neighbours and was eager to help those in need. Early in the morning she would collect the eggs and milk the cow, in the afternoon mend the nets and at night she sat at her spinning-wheel while Sheena boasted about her Dublin days - the splendid villa with servants and coaches, and visits to the opera or concerts; and this seemed more strange to the child than any fairy story.

Sheena suffered from isolation, she missed her husband's presence, and the rough Atlantic storms drove her to despair. Finally a fever forced her to stay in bed and as no doctor lived anywhere near the village, and the neighbours believed the fever was faked, Isabel had to nurse her and carry the burden of cleaning and cooking, as well as looking after the animals.

Fortunately Brendan had left enough peat for the fire and the larder was well-stocked. The bed stood in the kitchen and every evening Isabel asked her mother to tell stories. How differently did Sheena reflect on her experience of Dublin's society in her present state of health. She painted pictures of a jealous and ambitious crowd, of shallow entertainment, rivals in love, dissipation and lavish waste, lack of compassion, hurtful gossip and the gap between rich and poor.

Isabel listened. She tried to imagine what was meant by going to a ball, wearing dresses made of silk and dancing through the night. When Brendan returned he brought her a pretty new dress, a warm shawl for his wife and plenty of fresh fish. While he stayed he repaired storm damage, thatched the roof and filled the larder. He even brought medicine for Sheena and before he left he threw a parcel on her bed and disappeared. Sheena opened it only when her daughter was asleep and in the flickering firelight she unwrapped a polished mirror. How long had she not seen her face...fearfully she looked at herself: a stranger stared back at her. Matted hair, sunken cheeks and feverish eyes, that was all that was left of her beauty. She began to understand her husband. What would he feel when he saw her like this? She had been the Belle of the City, rich and young, wooed by many, spoilt by loving parents. When she ran away with him she had no idea what life was like for most people. She could neither cook nor clean, was incapable of lighting a fire or mending a net. The small cottage soon lost its attraction for the lovers and it was only Isabel, this extraordinary child, who helped her to adjust slowly. It was for the sake of the child that she learnt to milk the cow, bake bread, gut and fry fish, keep the place clean. The serene look in Isabel's face, her joy and gratitude were reward for Sheena. But she was ill-equipped for the life of a fisherman's wife. It was only her experience of having a bonny child that made her realise what pain she had inflicted on her own parents when she had left, in secret, what seemed to her now a totally different world.

Her joy in Isabel grew. This child greeted everyone she met with a delighted expectation, even total strangers. Whenever some foreign vessel entered the harbour it was always Brendan's house to which the sailors came first. Isabel used to stretch her small hands out to greet them and later ran on her short legs right into their arms, give them her biscuits and babble in Gaelic. When she grew older all rough talk or curses would pause in her presence, stolen eggs were returned and fighting stopped. If her parents warned her to be careful with strangers she quoted the rune of hospitality: 'Often, often, often, does Christ come in the form of a stranger.' Isabel had no fear of darkness or thunder. If she had to fetch peat in the dark she called the hobgoblin, the sprite who lived behind the stable. If the cow sickened she asked his advice and followed it faithfully, mixing vinegar and chopped-up herbs with the fodder; the hens were given nettles blended with their grain to yield more eggs and she spoke the right prayer when a calf was to be born.

Where had Isabel received such wisdom? The child had spoken to invisible beings from the time she learned to talk, and if she was asked how she understood the language of Spanish sailors she said: 'From earlier times.' Indeed there was no language she didn't comprehend and the door to every heart opened up for her.

As Sheena was lying on her sickbed it began to dawn on her that her own life, her whole destiny, the flight from Dublin, the secret wedding, yes even the loneliness of this godforsaken place had been essential in order to give life to this rare being. She remembered the brilliant star that stood in the west during the night Isabel was conceived: Jupiter, star of wisdom. What a baptism it had been! News of her elopement from the capital, of her fame and beauty, eye-witness accounts of the child's luminous glow had spread like wildfire, and the church was packed. Afterwards everyone present swore that the baby had smiled at them personally. Sheena felt embarrassed by the money people had given her, unused as she was to poverty.

For a long time Sheena looked in the mirror. It gave her answers to the painful question: why she had to lose her wealth and fame. The noble Frank Fitzgerald had asked for her hand, her parents adored him like a son and had promised him their elegant home, but she could not bear his truthfulness; he never flattered her and once seeing her in front of a mirror he had called: 'Sheena, I love you without paint. Be yourself!' She had not forgiven him. As a consequence she was today Mrs Malone and not Lady Fitzgerald. Now it was too late for remorse, the mirror spoke the truth. Would the looking-glass have power to destroy Isabel's innocence if she beheld her beauty? It had been a mirror that spoilt her fortune, but it had also given her self-knowledge and truth; it had shattered the last of her illusions, under no circumstance must it harm her daughter. She hid the mirror and fell into a feverish sleep.

Every morning Isabel used to come to her mother with the Bible and read to her. On this morning Sheena asked for the letter to the Corinthians. It was the 12th verse, chapter 13 she wanted to hear and Isabel read: 'For now we see in a glass darkly; but then face to face: now I am known in parts; but then shall I know even as also I am known. And now abideth faith, hope, love, these three; but the greatest of them is love.'

From this day on Isabel observed a change in her mother; her eyes regained lustre and she no longer bewailed her fate. During the long evenings Sheena prepared her child for a future without her and whenever she now spoke of Dublin it was to teach her names and places, sober instructions about life in the capital, patterns of behaviour so very different from that in the village. Up to now pride had prevented Sheena from mixing with neighbours, not even Brendan's mother had been invited. All that changed, and, full of expectation, Isabel prepared for her grandmother's visit, baking pancakes, picking flowers and helping her mother to wash and brush her hair. Precious driftwood was placed on the fire and the best cups laid out. Grandmother Malone hesitated on the threshold, steeling herself against the usual reproaches. But instead she heard a warm welcome, and the three women celebrated together. Before the visitor left Sheena said almost inaudibly: 'Forgive me, mother Malone.'

Rumours of the transformation in the fisherman's hut spread like lightning, and, one by one people came to see the patient. A teacher brought fine books for Isabel to read aloud, and neighbours asked whether they could help. A fiddler played for her, and before he left Sheena asked him what he knew of druidic wisdom about the sin of pride. The bard said: 'The three greatest sins are falsehood, perjury and pride, but pride is the worst sin of all.' Sheena nodded and thanked him.

It was Isabel's 14th birthday and her mother prepared a surprise. She unwrapped the mirror, placed all her own jewellery around it and lit a tall candle. The child was enchanted. Before she could reach out for the looking-glass Sheena spoke about the magic power within the shining glass. 'Whenever you look into this mirror you will see *me* as I was at your age. Keep the secret, for it only works as long as *you* look into it. As you grow older the picture will change. Take great care of it.' Reverently Isabel lifted the glass and there she saw a most beautiful face, radiant blue eyes, red-golden hair and a luminous skin. Isabel was enchanted. 'No wonder father loved you! You look like a princess.' And she danced around the room clasping her

gift in her arms. When Brendan arrived he was told of the
secret and understanding lit up his face. He had a lovely
dress and a new coat for Isabel, but the news he brought
was grim. The English army had terrorised the citizens of
Dublin and he believed more unrest would follow. He left
more medicines behind for Sheena and ample provisions,
promising another visit soon. He too had noticed the new
warmth and understanding in his wife.

During the winter Sheena grew weaker and she had to
fight for breath. Isabel longed for warmer weather and an
early spring; when it came at last she went out to pick the
first wild flowers and laid them on her mother's bed. Two
red patches burned on her cheeks, a sign of imminent
death. Sheena took Isabel's hands into her own and spoke
the Invocation of the Graces, as every mother was wont to
do before a child left home.

Invocation of the Graces

I bathe thy palms
In showers of wine,
In the lustral fire,
In the seven elements,
In the juice of rasps,
In the milk of honey,
And I place the nine pure choice graces
In thy fair fond face,
The grace of form,
The grace of voice,
The grace of fortune,
The grace of goodness,
The grace of wisdom,
The grace of charity,
The grace of choice maidenliness,
The grace of whole-souled loveliness,
The grace of goodly speech.

Dark is yonder town,
Dark are those therein,
Thou art the brown swan,
Going in among them.
Their hearts are under thy control,
Their tongues are beneath thy sole,
Nor will they ever utter a word
To give thee offence.

A shade art thou in the heat,
A shelter art thou in the cold,
Eyes art thou to the blind,
A staff art thou to the pilgrim,
An island art thou in the sea
A fortress art thou in the desert,
Health art thou to the ailing.

The best hour of the day be thine,
The best day of the week be thine,
The best week of the year be thine,
The best year in the son of God's domain be thine.

Peter has come and Paul has come,
James has come and John has come,
Muriel and Mary Virgin has come,
Uriel the all-beneficent has come,
Ariel the beauteousness of the young has come,
Gabriel the seer of the Virgin has come,
Raphael the prince of the valiant has come,
And Michael the chief of the hosts has come,
And Jesus Christ the mild has come,
And the Spirit of true guidance has come,
And the King of kings has come on the helm,
To bestow on thee their affection and their love,
To bestow on thee their affection and their love.

Exhausted, Sheena fell back on her pillow. The fire burned low and it was very still, the stars shone faintly; it was the hour of Saturn. There was a knock at the door and the priest entered. 'This is the end of the great spring tide and with the ebb a happy death is promised to you, Mrs Malone. Are you ready for the last anointing?' She nodded and the holy rites were performed in age-old tradition, giving renewed strength to Sheena.

When grandmother Malone was called Isabel was freed from nursing and she ran out to the harbour and watched the turn of the tide. Looking out to the horizon she saw her father's boat sail slowly against the wind. She made her way to the jetty and helped tie up the ropes. Brendan was relieved that he had not come too late. Together they carried his provisions inside and he found Sheena serene and with an unearthly beauty. All selfishness had burnt itself out and their last days together were full of peace. Brendan promised to sail with Isabel to Cork, from where a coach would take her to Dublin.

The child took her mirror and asked: 'Will this glass keep its magic?' Her mother assured her that even after her death it would keep its power, as long as she believed in it. That was a great comfort, for now she would be without the one person who had been with her every day of her life. 'Whenever you look into the mirror, yes, even if you just think of me, I will be with you, here and in the city,' Sheena promised.

Her last hours were blessed indeed and Brendan saw with amazement how his wife had won the hearts of the village folk. At the funeral a place of honour was given to the stranger who had become one of the good people during the last months of her life.

Isabel packed her bundle and sailed to Cork where her father paid for the coach to Dublin. Everything was new to her: the landscape, the people, the accent and the sensation of travel. Her thoughts were with her mother and she held the bag containing the mirror and jewellery close to her heart. Without any difficulty she found the elegant house with the two slender pillars and the fan-light over the door. She knocked with the brass handle and a gentlemen opened. 'Sheena! Are you young forever? Where have you been hiding, with the fairies?'
'No, Sheena is in the Land of Truth and I am her daughter Isabel. I have greetings for Frank Fitzgerald.'
'I am Frank Fitzgerald, and you are most welcome in your own house, step in,' and he took her bundle, handed it to a servant and ordered tea. The house was beautiful and luxurious, the drawing room had a bright log fire, pictures in gilded frames looked down from the walls, silk curtains filtered the afternoon light and on the thick carpet stood a Celtic harp. So this was her mother's home, this was what she had exchanged for the dark cottage by the sea.

Tears welled up in her eyes and Frank gave her time to compose herself. He too needed a moment to gather his thoughts. This child was even more beautiful than Sheena; she had a purity of soul not easily found in cities. Strong hot tea and fresh cream cakes revived Isabel and then followed one of those rare conversations which build bridges effortlessly and reach a profound level of understanding. It was as if they had known each other for ever.

In the weeks that followed Frank showed Isabel the city. She conquered Dublin by foot and with their private coach, meeting many of Frank's friends, but she had no inkling of the deep impression she made. She learnt about the brutal suppression of Irish culture by the

English, the suffering of the population, the suppressed hate and the many conspiracies and wild plans by rebels. The few sensible and cautious members of society warned that any rebellion would cause a bloodbath and would worsen the situation. The all-powerful empire stood behind the well-armed English army, while the Irish had no weapons to speak of. Frank was cool-headed and worked hard to strengthen the inner union and spiritual traditions of the country.

During the hot days of August a disaster occurred. Some English soldiers had thrown dead horses into the Liffey, polluting the purity of this holy river. An angry mob gathered near the bridge, collecting stones as missiles against the redcoats, and an officer yelled: 'Shoot the rabble!' But before the rifles were loaded Frank fought his way towards the front and cried: 'Save the innocent! Let me explain.' He was arrested at once while friends ran to warn Isabel of what had happened. They implored her to come to the courthouse and save Frank from certain death. They knew what British justice was like.

Isabel looked at her simple dress. She had refused to accept city clothes and she knew that everything depended now on the right appearance. Frank had given her a key to her mother's room but so far she had not used it. This was the moment to play the lady and pretend to be an adult. Resolutely she turned the key, the door opened and she found herself face to face with Sheena, a full-length picture it seemed, fully alive, just as she knew it from the magic mirror. Abruptly she changed direction, searching for a wardrobe. The curtain was drawn, only a little light filtered through but she groped her way towards a big wardrobe and its creaking doors opened slowly. A second time Isabel stared at a picture of her mother and her hands flew up to her face. The picture did the same, and only then she realised she was staring at herself in her homely dress.

With beating heart she fumbled among the frocks and pulled out a black one which was a little too long but otherwise fitted reasonably well. She also found a black hat and gloves. By now Frank's friend had the coach ready and she climbed in, still in a state of shock. The rhythm of clattering horses' hooves calmed her nerves until unexpectedly the voice of Sheena spoke within: 'Even if you just think of me I will be with you here and in the city.' New courage streamed through her and when they arrived at the courthouse she lost no time, hurried through the gate and up to the judicial tribunal where Frank stood chained between two soldiers. A judge with a white wig faced him, an officer demanded death by hanging. Fearlessly Isabel crossed the floor and confronted the bench. People in the gallery bent forward to see who had entered unannounced. Later, everywhere in Dublin's pubs and marketplaces the story was told how the apparition had seemed like a black angel, a fury, or like a saint.

Calling out in a clear voice Isabel Malore said: 'The rivers of Ireland are holy and we revere their water. Not in a thousand years have they been polluted and he who wants to rule Ireland has to respect our rivers. The people want no revolution, they came to protect our oldest right in the land and demand that the dead horses are cleared from the Liffey. The man you accuse is an advocate of peace. If you hang him then there will be mutiny on a scale Dublin has never seen before. In the name of the Father, the Son and the Holy Spirit I plead for justice.'

Stunned by this astonishing witness, the judge seemed at a loss for words and the onlookers in the gallery pleaded 'Mercy, mercy!' That very moment a messenger entered calling out: 'People are marching towards the garrison with burning torches! Our troops are in danger!' A hammer fell, the judge stood up. 'Quiet in Court. Will the accused explain whether he planned this attack on the garrison?' Frank Fitzgerald answered with a strong voice: 'I did not, your Worship.' 'Is it true that you are a peacemaker?' 'Yes it is. For years I have worked with the moderates to achieve an understanding,' and lifting his right hand he added: "All of my life I have represented peace and that is the truth, may God be my witness.' Within a few minutes of consultation the judge declared: 'The case is dismissed. Take off the chains.' The crowd cheered and Frank was carried shoulder high so that Isabel could hardly follow. The day's work was not yet done, there still remained the danger of a riot. To celebrate the judge's decision Frank charged his friends with the task of stopping the attack on the garrison. His messengers arrived in time, a large bonfire was lit outside town and patriotic songs were sung.

Isabel sat quietly in the drawing-room while Frank paced restlessly up and down. Taking a deep breath he finally stood still in front of her and asked: 'Who are you? Who gave you this strength and wisdom?' She looked up and answered thoughtfully: 'Even as a small child I used to look at my two hands and know that these lines did not come from this present life, they are older and I brought them with me. Why should I have been afraid of the judge? They can't do more than kill me and next time we would face each other again and justice would win in the end.' Frank nodded. 'Something similar has been familiar to me as well, but do you not know for sure *who* you have been?' 'For a long time I didn't. Only when you gave me the book of Lismore in which the life of Saint Bride is depicted, some pictures emerged deep inside of me which made sense of my feelings. All the heroes of Ireland came into her monastery in Kildare. Kings and bishops talked with me then. Why should I be afraid of Englishmen?' Then Frank laughed and all previous tension was released. 'Rather the English are afraid of you!'

The child sat before him in her black dress and he realised that something had changed, her face was no longer that of a child, a new and mature confidence radiated from her. Quite unexpectedly Isabel remarked: 'I guess that monasteries have no mirrors.' Frank was puzzled and she explained: 'In her last illness Sheena gave me a round mirror and said it possessed magic powers. Every time I looked into it the glass would show me the face of Sheena just as she had been at my age, the picture would grow with me, and I believed her. It was always dark in our cottage and nobody owned a mirror in the village. It had been a gift from my father and looking back now I believe it changed her life, made her gentle and forgiving. Today, when I entered her room for the first time I saw myself life-sized. It was a shock, a wholesome shock, it helped me to grow up.'

'Your mother was surrounded by mirrors, and when her parents gave the house to me I removed all of them except the ones in her room. Once I dared to criticise her for her vanity and she never forgave me; that's why I lost her. We ought never to judge others. Perhaps Sheena told you the story of the magic mirror in order to save you from vanity.'

'One night I listened to my parents when they thought I was asleep and I heard my mother confess her foolishness and add that the flight from Dublin, the loss of riches, the loneliness and poverty had all been necessary so that I could be born. It was around that time that her isolation ended and she became accepted by the neighbours.'

A servant entered and announced the visit of Mor MacNeil, the bard, famous in Scotland and Ireland. Wine was served and the day's event talked over. 'It's not the English occupation that is the greatest danger, there are some good men among them,' he explained, 'the army will leave in the end though it may take a long time. Freedom will come to Ireland eventually, but beware of the false priests who destroyed the Celtic church and exchanged the spirit of Saint John for the power of Saint Peter. We are in danger of forgetting the truth that we return to earth again and again until a new heaven and a new earth have been created. Our ancient songs and myths are being lost, the belief in Brigid the goddess is discouraged, she who rules like Sophia or Demeter is no longer worshipped.

Only Brigid, the handmaid of Mary and midwife of Jesus, is still remembered, unforgotten is Saint Brigid from Kildare. She returns in every generation and her song is the song for Isabel who saved our friend Fitzgerald from death.'

The bard bowed before Isabel and she listened with heightened understanding to the verses of Hail Brigid, known to every child in the land. Frank took the Book of Lismore into his hands; he was moved deeply when he spoke: 'I had no inkling of the meaning which the life history of this saint, who brought true faith to the green land, had for you. She was a nun but you are not and I beg you to accept this green dress from me because tonight we want to celebrate.'

Soon the house filled with guests, candles were lit, tables laid with sparkling silver and crystal, flowers arrived and Isabel danced into the room like a child. Mor MacNeill gave the toast: 'You are a true daughter of the Celtic people and your beauty radiates out over the just and the unjust, over the good and the wicked. Today you saved the life of *one*, soon you will go down on your knees for dozens of us and the Liffey will turn red with blood. Yet nothing can prevent the victory of truth. In the life of each one of us, past and future lives hold their sway. I drink this toast to the truth and that we may recognise each other in all future times. We drink to Brigid in all her forms, we drink to the heroine of today, to Isabel Malore.' All glasses were raised and the wine sparkled. The bonfire was still burning on the hill outside the city and no redcoat dared to walk abroad this night.

(The events of this story are fictional but reflect the historic fact that England ruled over Ireland for 800 years. What was suffered in the way of hunger, poverty and indignity can be compared with the holocaust of the Jews, as an English MP confessed recently in Parliament. Even today the conflict continues in Ulster.)

12. The Luckless One

Long, long ago there lived a man in a pleasant village amidst the ever fresh and green meadows of Ireland. All around him lived serene and contented people who felt that each day bright and beautiful things happened, yet for this man nothing came right. If he had work to do he grumbled that it was too heavy on him, if he had no work he complained he had no money, and so he was simply called the Luckless One, and he didn't like that name at all. Finally he went to a wise woman who suggested he ought to visit the Old Man at the End of the World who knew an answer to every question.

So the Luckless One set off and walked and walked for a day, a week and a year till he came to a wolf who looked exceedingly miserable. 'Where are you going to?' the wolf asked him.

'I am going to the Old Man at the End of the World, he has an answer to every question.'

'Please ask him why I am always hungry and what I can do?' The man promised he would.

He walked and walked for a day, a week and a year till he came to a withered tree whose leaves were falling off while all other trees were thriving. 'Where are you going to?' asked the tree. 'I am going to the Old Man at the End of the World, he has an answer to every question.' 'Please ask him why I am shrivelling up when all other trees are thriving.' The man promised he would.

He walked and he walked for a day, a week and a year until he came to a fine house in which there dwelled a friendly woman. 'Where are you going?' she asked. 'I am going to the Old Man at the End of the World, he has an answer to every question.' 'Please ask him why I am so lonely,' and the man promised. Before he left she cooked a delicious meal for him, gave him a soft warm bed and a good breakfast.

He walked and he walked for a day, a week and a month and then he was at the End of the World where he put all his questions to the Old Man and got an answer for each one.

With wings on his feet he set off for home and soon he reached the fine house where he received a warm welcome. 'What did the Old Man say?' she asked. 'Oh, he said: when a man comes to your house you should marry him and you will never be lonely.' ' You are a man and you've come to my house, please marry me.' 'Oh no, to me the Old Man said I would find my happiness on the way, I simply have to go on.' She cooked him a fine meal, gave him a soft bed and sadly she let him go.

The Luckless One sped back till he arrived at the withered tree that had lost all its leaves and whispered hoarsely: 'What did the Old Man say?' 'Ah, he said, at the roots of your trunk lies a big iron box full of gold pieces and if somebody digs it up then your roots will reach fresh water and you will be well.' 'There is a spade here, please dig up the box so that I may drink again!' whispered the tree pleadingly. 'Oh no, that I cannot do; to me the Old Man said I would find happiness on the way, I have to be off.'

With more and more haste the Luckless one hurried on till he came to the wolf who looked even hungrier than before. 'What did the Old Man say to you?' 'Ha, he gave a funny answer! He said: The dinner stands in front of you!' And the wolf ate and ate until nothing was left of the Luckless One, and he licked his lips well contented.

13. The Birds' Last Supper

It had been a long and cold winter, followed by a wet and late spring. The small brotherhood of monks on the west coast of Ireland were facing starvation. The monks were chilled to the bone in their stone-built cells, their songs and prayers sounded weaker by the day and the cowls hung loosely around the body of abbot and monk likewise. Beyond the monastery walls, built against Vikings and pirates, the layfolk lived with their wives and children in close communion with the holy men of God. Every morning their chieftain sent a trusted man to the barn where the grain was stored, to receive their rations. The monk responsible for the distribution held perhaps the most important office in the community and the grainstore was guarded day and night. From the isle of Iona sacks with white sand had been brought by boat and sprinkled around the barn to protect it from mice or rats as no such creature could ever step across it. It is a custom observed still by a few pious people.

It was the night before Beltane, the spring festival, when in heathen times the seed for a new fire had been carried from Tara to every hamlet, but there was no festive mood among the monks. All through the night the person responsible for the corn had tossed and turned. Only towards morning did he fall into a light slumber, after deciding to cut the food for the birds which so far had been given grain daily. The spectre of starvation was now all too close.

Suddenly awoken by a slight noise he watched with fear and trembling: a man stood inside the horrerum or grainstore, filled his hands with grain and walked to the door, which stood open. Shaking violently the monk arose. In his very bones he knew that this was no thief and no stranger. Outside thousands of birds filled the air with the beating of their wings, yet not a cry, not a song could be heard. The figure in a cowl stepped to a flat stone and began to read Mass and prepare Holy Communion. When it came to the sharing of bread in the Last Supper every one of the birds came close and took the blessed body of the Lord.

When the Amen had been spoken the monk fell on his knees and the Saviour turned to him and said: 'If you will no longer feed these creatures who are my brothers they will all die of hunger. I gave them the Last Supper today. Where is your faith?' and he vanished. When the trusted man came to fetch the rations for the lay people he noticed a strange light surrounding the horrerum, yet the monk did not speak a single word. Instead he took two handfuls of grain and with a gesture of blessing fed the numerous birds who came to him, as he did every morning.

The grain did not diminish. Enough was left for the sowing of the new season, none of the brothers died, the community survived. Many people who visit this part of Ireland today, long after the monastery has gone, ask the people in wonder: 'Why is it that the birds sing sweeter here than at any other place on the green island?'

14. How Heavy is a Snowflake?

An old Celtic legend tells the story of the wren and the owl. The first snow had fallen and the island in the middle of the loch within the centre of Ireland was coated with a soft, white blanket under which all life seemed buried. Yet from a hollow between branches of an ancient holy oak tree a tiny voice could be heard, and after an interval of silence one could observe the dignified and slow movement of a dark brown, soft-feathered sphere, complete with tufted ears and claws, leaving its nest in the crown of the oak. The gold-rimmed pupils rolled about, the owl was meditating. Then a deep rough voice rang out over the snowscape, answered by a faint twittering.

'How heavy is a snowflake, brother Owl?' asked the wren.
'A snowflake weighs nothing, my little Wren, absolutely nothing you could weigh or measure', answered the owl.
'Then how come I saw what I saw on this winter morning?'
'What did you see on this winter morning which made you dare to wake me from my deepest sleep, you smallest of all birds?'
'When I dreamt my winter dream in my small nest a snowflake melted on my breast and woke me up. Outside a light snow fell and I began to count. First there were thousands, then hundreds of thousands of flakes. Oh wise brother Owl, after I counted one million and three flakes the branch broke just in front of my nest, and still the snow kept falling. What now is the weight of a single snowflake here in the heart of the wood in the heart of Ireland?'

Beaten in this debate the owl retreated silently and slowly, and to this very day folk like to tell the story on long winter evenings. To this very day nobody has found an answer to the question of the clever wren. But whosoever contemplates the riddle may find courage in his heart to stand up to the great and mighty in this world. If they try to convince us that we carry no weight we may remember the tiny wren.

15. The Worst of all Weathers

At the time of Ciara of Clonmacnoise there were two devoted monks whom the saint asked to bring thatch for his church, and it was a Saturday of all days when Beogin and Naoi took their sickles and went along to the river Shannon and worked hard till they had cut enough green-topped rushes to fill their little curragh. But before they completed the task they heard the bells ringing out for vespers and resolved to wait and not return till Monday, to keep the day of the Lord.

That night they suffered greatly, having neither bed nor roof, neither food nor fire and only their hot prayers kept them alive at all, because a storm came upon them, more violent than any fragile human being had ever felt before. First there was rain, then snow and rain again, hail and frost, followed by gales of wind, icy rain and a hard frost which touched every hair on their heads until it was frozen stiff.

Yet such was their faith that the spark of life did not go out, and not only did they find themselves still breathing when morning dawned but they had undergone an initiation of a special kind: suddenly they could understand the language of birds. Here is the conversation which Beogin recorded and Naoi witnessed as true. Leithin the eagle and the little lay-hen spoke thus: 'Leithin, do you ever remember the like of this morning or of last night to have come into thy knowledge before?' She lamented her cold state pitifully, sadly, grievously, and the eagle answered: 'I do not remember that I ever saw or heard the like or the equal of them since the world was created; or did you ever hear of such weather?'
'There are people who do remember,' said the bird.
'Who are they?'
'Dubhchosach, the black-footed one of Ben Bulen in County Sligo.'

'That vast stag of the deluge, the hero of oldest memory of all his generation in Ireland? Confusion on thee! Now although the stag be far away from me I shall go and see him so that I may get knowledge.' The eagle flew off.

Finally Leithin found the swift-footed stag scratching himself against a bare oak rampike, saluted him and said:

> Well for you. O Blackfoot, on Ben Bulben high,
> Many moors and marshes, leap you lightly by.
> Tell me stag high-headed, saw you ever fall
> Such a night and morning? You remember all.

The stag answered:

> I will give you answer Leithin wise and gray
> Such a night and morning never came my way.

'Tell me, Blackfoot, what is thy age?'
'I shall tell thee. I remember this oak when it was a sapling and I was born at the foot of it and the oak grew till it was a giant tree and I used to scratch myself against it until I became a mighty great stag and this oak a shapeless rampike, but I never heard tell a tale of a night like last night.'

The eagle returned and told the lay-hen what he had suffered in wet and cold without getting an answer. 'I know that Dubghoire of Clonfert, the black vulture, is older, he should know.'

The eagle flew to Clonfert and saw a splendid bird but its feathers were white with age. 'O Dubghoire, you came from the nest that Brigit blessed, tell me, did you ever experience such bad weather as yesterday?'
'Since Lugh the God of Light reigned I have never seen weather like yesterday neither on sea nor land,' answered Dubghoire, and Leithin flew back.

Heavy were his wings when he returned but the lay-hen gave no peace.

'Even if that vulture did not know, there is still Goll the salmon; he is certain to know if anyone in the world could know and he swims at Ballyshannon and is called the Blind One. Ask him if he saw worse weather.'

'It is hard for me to fly there but I would really like to know about this thing,' said Leithin, and he searched out the salmon near the ford.

'It is to thee, O Blind One, that I have come to ask, how far does thy memory go back?' The salmon answered: 'As for my memory, that is a long one, it is not easy to reckon it, there is no-one as old as me. I remember Patrick coming to Ireland, I remember the Fir Bolg and people from Greece coming and I remember such cold that when I leapt into the air the water was frozen hard and this pool turned into one flag of ice, and a bird of prey pecked and bore away my clear blue eye. To me it was not a pleasant world.'

'Well now, did you ever remember a worse night than yesterday?'

'Indeed I saw such a night and morning, the coming of the deluge when great showers fell and the rain never stopped till only four men and four women survived and that was Noah and his wife and Sem, Cam and Japhet and their wives, the crew of the Ark. God left nobody undestroyed but these and that was by far the worst morning that I ever saw, worse than the morning you speak of.'

The two monks returned and told Kieran the news, word for word. Since that time every Irishman begins his conversation with the weather, and if a stranger is patient enough he might hear the story of the worst weather.

This version came from Douglas Hyde, the storyteller.

16.   The Tale of the Cauldron

There was once a farmer's wife in the Highlands and she
had a cauldron. There used to come a fairy wife every day
to get the cauldron. She used to say nothing when she
came, but she would seize the cauldron and the housewife
would say:

A smith is entitled to coals,
In order cold iron to heat;
A cauldron's entitled to bones,
And to be sent home whole.

The fairy used to come back every day with the cauldron
full of flesh and bones.

One day the good wife was going over on the ferry to
Castletown and so she said to her husband: 'If thou wilt say
to the fairy wife what I say, I will go to Castletown.' 'Oh I
will say what thou dost,' he said, 'certainly it is I who will.'
'Well then,' said she, 'I will go.' And off she went.

He was left alone, and so he began to work. He was
spinning a heather thatching rope in order to bind the
thatch on the house, when he saw the woman coming - a
shimmering came from her feet, and she moved along like
a fairy. He became afraid of her. He stopped working,
went into the house and shut the door. He was so
frightened he did not say a single word to the fairy,
although he had promised that he would. When the fairy
came to the door she did not find it open and he would
not open it to her. She went onto the roof above the
smoke-hole. The cauldron gave two leaps and at the third
leap it went out through the roof of the house; she seized
it and went off with it.

Night came but the cauldron didn't appear. Why did it not come? Because the good man had not said to the fairy what the good wife used to say. The wife came across the ferry but she could not see anything of the cauldron in the house. She asked where the cauldron was.

'Well then, I don't care where it is,' said her husband. 'Never did I take such fear as I took at the fairy woman. I took fear and I shut the door. She went up onto the roof above the smoke hole. The cauldron then gave two leaps and on the third leap away it went out through the roof of the house. She seized it and went off with it and came back with it no more.'

'GOOD FOR NOTHING WRETCH! What hast thou done? It is two people who will be badly off now, thyself and myself.'

'She will come tomorrow with it.' 'No, she will not come.'

She hastily got herself ready and off she went to the fairy hillock. There was nobody within but a couple of grey-haired old men who were asleep. It was after dinner time and the rest of the fairies were out in the gathering night. In she went softly and without speaking, without even blessing the people of the fairy-dwelling. She saw the cauldron on the floor and picked it up to take away with her. She found it heavy and it was full of remnants of food. As she went out the cauldron came in collision with the door post. It gave an awful shriek and the grey-haired old men awoke. When they saw her leaving, taking the cauldron with her, one of them rose and said:

> O dumb wife, o mute wife!
> Who camest upon us from the Land of the Dead!
> Thou man who art on the top of the fairy-dwelling,
> Let loose the Black and slip the Fierce!'

The good wife went off at her utmost speed, and he was too old and could not keep up with her. The good wife kept the remnants of food in order that she could throw the scraps to Black and Fierce. The man who was on the top of the fairy-dwelling let the two dogs, Black and Fierce, loose. She had not got far away when she heard the rustling and pattering of the dogs coming, a cause of fear and of horror. She put her hand into the cauldron and took the lid out of it and threw them a quarter of all that was in it. The dogs turned their attention to that for a while. She made off as fast as she could, not knowing how long the bones would last her, or whether she would get home before the dogs caught her.

Again she saw them coming and she threw them another piece, when they were closing in on her. Away she went, footing it as well as she could, knowing that the cause of fear and of horror was not far behind her. When she was getting near her home farm they were closing on her again. She tipped the cauldron upside down and there she left them with all that there was in it.

Away she flew home, running and leaping. The dogs at the home farm heard the good wife coming and they struck up a barking, when they saw the fairy dogs. The fairy dogs took fright when they heard the farm dogs barking and they took themselves off, with their tails between their hind legs. Never again did the fairy woman come to collect the cauldron. Never did the fairies bring trouble on the good wife.

This version of the ancient legend of the Scottish Gael comes from J G McKay

17. The King and the Beautiful Lamp

Once upon a time when tin was the metal used to fashion most vessels and utensils there lived a tin merchant who was an artist in his trade. He earned his living by travelling from place to place and selling his wares. On his back he carried not only all the tools needed but also a tent which he would put up wherever he wished to stay longer and the good folk welcomed him most warmly as he was honest and wise.

One day he came into a country where he had always been able to sell his very best pieces for a fair price, yet this time nobody bought anything at all. His customers seemed sad and dispirited, unwilling to engage in conversation. Finally he reached the last house of the town where a wise woman lived to whom he had sold some of his finest masterpieces. Even she shook her head: 'Don't unpack your wares, there is not enough money for even a trinket, but come in and have a cup of tea.'

Glad to sit down, the merchant asked: 'What has happened here, tell me?'
'Our King has laid heavy taxes on us, he takes most of the grain and not enough is left to feed man nor beast, the miller has no corn, the baker no bread and all trade is crippled. Soon we will have to leave our country as beggars or starve to death.' 'But why not tell the King?' asked the traveller. 'We are too weak to stand up to him and his soldiers would not let us near in any case.' 'Thank you, now I know what to do!' The tin merchant took his pack and walked to the castle and put up his tent well within sight of the guards. He lit a fire, got out his tools and began working on a lamp.

It was a skilful and most intricately-designed lamp, the finest he had ever made and the pattern would throw beautiful shadows when the wick was burning. The guards saw the fire and came to chase him away. 'This road belongs to our King, how dare you ply your trade without a license?' Calmly he replied: 'That I will tell your King in person because it is for him that I work.' The guards were surprised and watched how the four sides were soldered together and burnished until they shone. Then the coach arrived with the King and he inquired what the merchant was doing. 'I have made a piece of art for the ruler of this country, yet there is one condition attached to the gift.' The King became curious, he stepped from the coach and looked at the lamp. Never before had he seen anything as beautifully made and he wished to purchase the lamp immediately. The tin merchant continued rubbing the metal until it was bright like a mirror. 'Is the lamp finished?' the King asked impatiently. 'Yes, this lamp is ready for a just King.' 'How much do you want for it?' 'It costs nothing except the promise not to show any anger and to solve the riddle of this lamp.' 'What is its secret?' 'The lamp reveals all weaknesses and faults of his Majesty's subjects.' 'Ah, that is a splendid gift! I promise not to show any anger. Here are four pieces of gold, a just King has to pay for good workmanship. I order you to remain till tomorrow so that I may test the lamp and see whether you have told the truth about it. Woe to you if you have deceived me.'

With great pride he carried the lamp into the castle and showed it to his wife. She clapped her hands with delight and ordered the servants to fill it with tallow and light it. Ah what a splendid sight! The shadows danced on the walls with their four distinct patterns and the hall glowed brightly as never before. The Queen ordered the table to be laid and the new lamp placed next to the

King. Hardly had his Majesty sat down when a stream of burning hot tallow ran over the tablecloth onto the King's trousers and the precious carpet.

'Fetch the villain who sold this rubbish to me! He shall suffer!' cried the infuriated King who felt the hot flow congeal on his trousers and burn his leg. While the servants ran to carry out the order the King remembered what he had promised and tamed his wrath. Calm and composed the merchant stood and listened to the accusations: 'This is a useless lamp, it had burned for less than ten minutes when the tallow ran out and ruined my table, my clothes and the carpet. Yet you claim it is the best lamp for a just King?'

'It is the finest lamp I have ever made and it is not my fault if it leaks. I bought the tin in your country. If the metal is inferior even the best artist cannot produce a good lamp. Ask the man who sold the tin.'

An order was given to the soldiers and as fast as the wind the shopkeeper was brought to the king.

'Did you sell tin to this merchant?' With shaking knees the man answered: 'Yes I did, he came today and bought a sheet of tin.' 'Look at this lamp made from your tin, it is defective and it is your fault that my table, my clothes and the carpet are ruined.' The man defended himself: 'O Majesty, if the tin is defective it is because of the foundry where I buy the raw material.'

The soldiers were sent to the owner of the foundry and as fast as the wind he arrived; his teeth were chattering with fear. 'Did you sell tin to this shopkeeper who made sheets of it to sell?' 'Yes, I own the only foundry here and I sold tin to the man.' Then it is your fault that the lamp is faulty which ruined the table, my clothes and the carpet.' 'Oh no, your Majesty, it is the fault of the bellows-maker. If the bellows are faulty then my fires won't burn strong enough and the tin is spoilt.'

So the soldiers galloped into the village and caught the man who made the bellows. 'Did you make the bellows sold to the owner of this foundry?' asked the King. 'Yes sir, I am the only bellows-maker in town.' 'Then it is your fault that the fires burnt poorly when the tin was smelted from which the metal sheets were made to fashion this lamp that spoilt the table, my clothes and the carpet.' 'Oh Majesty, it is not my fault that the bellows are faulty. I had to buy leather from the tannery and if the leather is of poor quality the bellows will be faulty.'

The soldiers galloped to fetch the tanner to court. 'Did you sell leather to the bellows-maker who is standing here?' 'Yes, O King, I sold him leather for his craft,' answered the tanner. 'Then it is your fault that the bellows are faulty that were used for the fire to smelt the tin and make sheets of metal for this lamp which ruined the table, the clothes and the carpet of your King!' The tanner stood his ground. 'No sir, I am not guilty. The farmer who sold me the skin of his cow is guilty. If the skin is poor no tanner can make good leather from it.'

Off rode the soldiers to collect the farmer and took him to the King. His face was ashen and yet he stood upright to listen to the accusations. 'Did you sell the skin of a cow to this tanner here?' the king demanded to know. 'Yes, your Majesty, I sold him the skin of one of my poor cows,' he replied. 'Then it is your fault that the bellows were faulty which blew the fire to smelt the tin and make the sheet of metal for this lamp which spoilt the table, my clothes and the carpet, as you can see with your own eyes.' 'Even if the skin was bad it is still not my fault.' 'Then whose fault is it, pray?' the king asked and expectantly all eyes turned to the farmer. 'It is your own fault, o King.' Fury filled the king, his veins stood out, he stepped forward – then suddenly he remembered his promise, controlled himself and inquired: 'How can it be MY fault?'

'There is corn growing in my field but most of it I have to hand over as taxes, and my wife and children and I have hardly enough left to feed ourselves and the cow. We are starving, the cow is starving and the skin of the beast is so wretched that no tanner could make good leather with it, nobody can make good bellows from the leather, no good fire can be coaxed into hot flames, no good metal can be smelted with a poor fire and if the tin is faulty the lamp will be faulty.'

It was very still and every eye was on the King. 'Indeed this is a magic lamp, it illuminated the weakness of my subjects but also my own weakness. What may I do in order to get a beautiful and well-made lamp?' The wise tin merchant answered: 'Look into the faces of your subjects, because there the reason can be seen plainly: it is hunger. Hungry people cannot make anything beautiful. The horses of your soldiers are better fed and consume more grain than any of your own people. This used to be a rich and prosperous country and will be so again if it is your Majesty's wish.' Before the King could reply, the Queen stepped forward: 'May I send for the cook and order a meal to be served to these, our guests?' A royal nod and the servants sped into the kitchen, a table was laid and a rich feast prepared for the farmer, the tanner, the bellows-maker, the smith and the tin maker, the King and Queen and our wise merchant.

When they had all eaten well the King spoke as follows: 'Though this lamp was faulty it has thrown new light on my task as a king. I promise to leave enough corn to the farmer so that his cow is well fed and produces good leather which will make strong bellows to blow hot fires to smelt the metal which will give the best sheets of tin to our wise and skilful maker of lamps.'

Each of the men received a basket of food for their wives and children. One basket, packed by the tin merchant himself with extra care, was taken to the last house in the town, to the woman who had disclosed the reason for the country's poverty.

Do you think that this could happen elsewhere? Just ask the tinker Duncan Williams who told the story, which he heard from his father's father before.

Sibylle Alexander

Sibylle Alexander was born in 1925 in Hamburg as the third child of a family of four. Her father was a judge and as he was a contributor to the journal 'European Conversations' Hitler dismissed him in 1933, which meant acute hardship but allowed the previously busy father to spend his time telling stories from the Brothers Grimm, to whose collection Dorothea Wild, wife of Wilhelm Grimm, (his great-aunt), had made a substantial contribution.

The family moved to Vienna in 1940 where the restrictions on him were lifted and a rich cultural life could be enjoyed. Sibylle formed a Spielschar or troupe of players which performed some of her own plays in hospitals, schools and to evacuees living along the Danube.

Before the Russians took Vienna in April 1945 she escaped to Hamburg where the British occupying forces appointed her to create the first free Radio Programme for children, Die Spieldose, in September 1945. With this her writing career began.

Later she studied German Literature, Theology and Philosophy of Education at Hamburg, Uppsala and Tübingen where she gained the equivalent of a First Class Honours Degree. She married in 1951 and has five children. Moving to Scotland in 1955 to teach at the Edinburgh Rudolf Steiner School, she was later offered a post as German Tutor at Moray House Teacher Training College and wrote three German Readers, (Oxford Press, Oliver and Boyd, Cassells).

Since 1980 she has toured Germany, Austria and Switzerland to lecture on Celtic themes, creating three collections for the Celtica series at Mellinger Verlag

Stuttgart, and the volumes Am Torffeuer erzählt, Der Mönch aus Iona, Der Harfenspieler, are very popular with adults and children. The stories were first written in English and have been told many times by her in both languages. She is a member of the International Storytelling Club, The Netherbow, Edinburgh, and belongs to the Border Storytellers.

Sibylle Alexander has seven grandchildren in Scotland and five in Germany

Galashiels, May 1999

Other books from Hawthorn Press

Beyond the Forest
Kelvin Hall
The Grail Quest is an archetypal story of the journey of humanity and of each person. Parzival's search for wholeness - passed down by generations of storytellers - is re-told vividly here by Kelvin Hall.

There is a Parzival in every one of us as we move from the innocence and naivety of forgetting, through courage and surrender, to love and redemption. Impaired by fear, bewilderment, loss and misunderstanding, we learn to trust the instinct of the heart as well as accepting the wisdom and support of others on the way.

This ancient story, told by Wolfram von Eschenbach in the Middle Ages, asks us why we restrain ourselves from asking the compassionate question. It shows how the result is our suffering and alienation, and that by engaging with the suffering of others, we acknowledge our own. This brings forth the possibility for transformation and renewal.

Because this is an initiation story, it will be especially useful to English and Drama teachers, storytellers and psychotherapists. This Parzival story is an essential part of the Steiner/Waldorf curriculum for Class 11 (17 year olds) and *Beyond the Forest* is the most accessible version for teenagers.

Kelvin Hall was first told the Parzival story by his future wife, Barbara. Storyteller-in-residence at Ruskin Mill, Gloucestershire, he is active in the British Storytelling Revival, winning the 'Liar of the Year' contest.

96pp; 216 x 138mm; 1 869 890 73 6; paperback; £8.99

Sing Me the Creation
Paul Matthews
This is an inspirational workbook of creative writing exercises for poets and teachers, and for all who wish to develop the life of the imagination. There are over 300 exercises for improving writing skills. Though intended for group work with adults, teachers will find these exercises easily adaptable to the classroom.

Paul Matthews, a poet himself, taught creative writing at Emerson College, Sussex.

224pp; 238 x 135mm; 1 869 890 60 4; paperback; £10.99

70 Years A-Growing
Jean Westlake
This book is the story of a magical life committed to organic and biodynamic gardening, and has been 70 years in the making.

Packed with practical gardening information and useful resources, it is also an enticing autobiography of 'muck and magic'. It follows the twists and turns of one family, from running a simple holiday home to the

121

accolade of having their produce recognised by Demeter and The Soil Association.
Full of delicious humour, quirky stories, and written in the wider context of a fascinating life, it will leave you feeling like a member of the family - desperate to return home and catch up with old friends.

Jean Westlake is also the author of the famous *Sandy Balls for All Seasons* and *Gypsy Caravan - a 100 years story*. She was televised in *Muck and Magic* in 1988.

70 Years A-Growing holds as much appeal for the wider public as it does for the organic and biodynamic specialist. Not only a mine of gardening information, it stands in its own right as an eminently enjoyable story of one family's relationship to the earth which gives them a living.

272pp; 246 x 189mm; 1 869 890 37 X; paperback; £14.99

Orders

Ordering information from:
Hawthorn Press
1 Lansdown Lane, Stroud, Gloucestershire
GL5 1BJ. United Kingdom
Tel: (01453) 757040   Fax: (01453) 751138
E-mail: hawthornpress@hawthornpress.com

If you have difficulties ordering from a bookshop you can order direct from:
Scottish Book Source Distribution
137 Dundee Street, Edinburgh
EH11 1BG
United Kingdom
Tel: (0131) 229 6800   Fax: (0131) 229 9070

All Hawthorn Press Titles are available in North America From:
Anthroposophic Press
3390 Route 9, Hudson,
NY 12534
U.S.A
Tel: (518) 851 2054   Fax (518) 851 2047